MARK RAINSLEY

PADDLE THE THAMES

A GUIDE FOR CANOES, KAYAKS AND SUPS

First published 2017

Published in Great Britain 2017 by Pesda Press
Tan y Coed Canol
Ceunant
Caernarfon
Gwynedd
LL55 4RN

ISBN 9781906095598

Contains Ordnance Survey data © Crown copyright and database right 2017

Maps by Bute Cartographic

Printed and bound in Poland, www.hussarbooks.pl

Foreword

An adventure in our own backyard is what we set off to find. With a passion for the outdoors and the water, we realised we didn't need to travel far. Just over an hour out of London, you find yourself standing at the source of the River Thames: a 215 mile-long river which starts from a spring and is marked by a stone in a field. The adventure we set ourselves was to stand up paddleboard the entire length of the Thames, from source to Southend-on-Sea.

We would be asked by many "Isn't the Thames dirty and polluted?". Spending eleven days and an average of nine hours a day on the river, and camping on the river banks ... our answer is "No", for the most part. We discovered it to be a river rich with wildlife, surrounded by beautiful countryside and the warmth of its communities, history and people. We encountered many interesting and friendly people, from those living on canal boats to kind lock keepers, children learning to kayak, fishermen perched on the riverbanks and ramblers walking at the same pace as we paddled; each of us talking about our journeys and our love of the river.

It was a privilege to be able to follow the transition of the river and its landscape and to do so in a unique way. What we discovered is how ordinary people can take part in the protection of such a beautiful resource. With many charities working hard to improve the quality of our river and the recreational use of it, there are many ways that we can all get involved. For us, this translated into becoming citizen scientists with Thames21 (www.thames21.org.uk), where we were trained to quickly and easily test the water quality for the Thames River Watch and to understand the issues surrounding plastic pollution.

How can you create your own river journey – for a day, a weekend or, as we did, along the entire length of the Thames? This guidebook is a perfect resource in helping you plan your route, providing you with all the details you need to know to have a fun, safe and adventurous paddle.

It really is a special river, one that we keep returning to time and again.

Michelle Ellison and Melanie Joe travelled the length of the River Thames by paddleboard in 2015, and in 2016 organised the first Thames River Relay www.thamesriverrelay.com.

Contents

Introduction

"Glide gently, thus forever glide,
O Thames! that other bards may see,
As lovely visions by thy side
As now, fair river! come to me."

Lines written near Richmond, upon the Thames, at Evening,
William Wordsworth, 1790

The River Thames is simply a fantastic place to paddle your canoe, kayak or paddleboard, whether touring, training, racing, expeditioning or just 'bimbling'. From its early reaches in the Cotswold Hills, through the Home Counties into London and far out beyond into the estuary, the river's surroundings are remarkably varied and diverse, yet always attractive and engaging. If your mental image of the Thames depicts an urban sewer, be prepared to be amazed; the water is clean, the banks are invariably green and naturalists describe the river's ecosystems as a 'wildlife superhighway'. This natural beauty is equalled by the human story which the Thames narrates; from locks, gardens and parks to mansions, abbeys, castles and palaces, the paddler is continuously immersed in what MP John Burns famously called "liquid history". The riverine Arcadia of willow-draped banks, back channels and islands celebrated in *Three Men in a Boat* and *The Wind in the Willows* was not a myth, and it still exists.

Is a paddler's guidebook to the Thames needed? Britain's best-known river might actually be the least-known by paddlers. The huge paddling population and numerous canoe clubs based along it belie a surprising fact; many of these paddlers aren't sure what is found up- and down-stream from their patch. In a river stretching 347km, this is both understandable and forgivable. However, there are other reasons for the relatively low numbers of paddlers encountered while enjoying the Thames. Information about where and how to launch is hard to come by, existing guides and media give the impression that the Thames is the preserve of powerboats and rowers, and finally, the perception often lingers that it isn't actually very attractive or interesting. This book sets out to redress these major omissions and misconceptions, and to reclaim John 'Rob Roy' MacGregor's river for paddlers. I hope that it helps you to enjoy many adventures on Britain's greatest river.

Mark Rainsley

About the Author

Mark Rainsley

Mark has spent three decades using paddlesport as a means of avoiding adulthood and responsibility. He is a fanatical paddler who has descended challenging whitewater rivers worldwide, and who is dedicated to exploring every nook and cranny of the UK's coast by sea kayak. He created the UK Rivers and UK Sea Kayak websites and is a prolific contributor to paddlesport magazines and other media. Mark authored the Pesda Press guidebooks *South West Sea Kayaking* and *River Wye Canoe and Kayak Guide* and has contributed to Pesda titles such as *English Whitewater* and *South East England & Channel Islands Sea Kayaking*.

The author. Photo | Eurion Brown.

Thames Whitewater?

The whitewater training and playing possibilities offered by the Thames' weirs have been researched by Chris Wheeler and Andy Jackson and are shared in *English Whitewater*, Pesda Press, 2014, ISBN 9781906095451.

Acknowledgements

In summer, pipe in hand, grandad would steer his canal barge *Comus* from Coventry down the canal to Oxford, downstream to London on the River Thames, and then all the way back again. Before wartime service, he had bought a German folding kayak from Harrods and explored the Thames with it. He was adamant that the Thames was the finest of all waterways; I have his stories to thank for my interest in the river.

Researching the Thames, dozens of friends paddled along; I told them they were only there to give me something to point the camera at, but in truth, paddling (and writing guidebooks) is just an excuse to hang out with them. I also loved paddling with my lovely wife Heather, my gorgeous daughter Ellen, and my dad, who may eventually forgive me for subjecting him to Central London in an open canoe.

The following folk provided expert input. Melanie Joe and Michelle Ellison were kind enough to write the Foreword. Russell Robson of the Environment Agency (Operational Waterways Team Leader) and Darren Knight of the Port of London Authority (Assistant Harbour Master Recreation) helpfully checked the advice to paddlers. Ian Holmes described his expeditions, and Andy Jackson of Thames Canoes contributed hire industry perspective. Steve Newton's students at Abingdon School gave feedback on their Duke of Edinburgh Award expeditions. Dr Lizzie Garnett supplied expertise for the Geology section.

Finally, thanks to Franco Ferrero at Pesda Press, Vicky Barlow for her great design work, Heather Hall and Ros Morley for their meticulous proofreading, and Don Williams of Bute Cartographic for the stunning maps.

Photographs

All photographs by Mark Rainsley, except where acknowledged in the captions.

📷 *Launching at Aston.*

Important notice – disclaimer

Canoeing, kayaking and other paddlesports, whether in a river or sea environment, have their inherent risks, as do all adventurous activities. This guidebook highlights some considerations to take into account when planning your own river journey.

While we have included a range of factors to consider, you will need to plan your own journey and within that ensure there is scope to be adaptable to local conditions; for example tides, weather and ever-changing river hazards. This requires knowing your own abilities, then applying your own risk assessment to the conditions that you may encounter. The varying environmental conditions along the River Thames mean that good judgement is required to decide whether to paddle or not.

The information within this book has been well researched. However, neither the author nor Pesda Press can be held responsible for any decision of whether to paddle or not and any consequences arising from that decision. A guidebook is no substitute for personal inspection at the time of paddling, and your own risk assessment and judgement. Your decision to paddle or not, and any consequences arising from that decision, is your responsibility.

Iffley Lock

Iffley COMMUNITY
SHOP CHURCHWAY IFFLEY VILLAGE
• Fresh Bread •
Fruit & Veg •
Fairtrade Produce •
Quality GROCERIES
• Biscuits. Savouries. etc •
Chilled Drinks • ICE CREAM
STAMPS & PARCEL POST SERVICE
Opening Mon. Tues. Thurs.
Hours Fri 9—5
Wed & Sat 9—1

Thames Highlights

We hope that this book will inspire you to explore and enjoy as much of this wonderful river as possible. However, here are just a few suggested highlights to get you started ...

Meadows, woods and hills

Places of natural beauty to enjoy from the water or venture ashore and explore.

Chimney Meadows Nature Reserve (Section 3)

Port Meadow (Section 4)

Wittenham Clumps (Section 6)

Goring Gap (Section 7)

Temple Meadow (Section 9)

Winter Hill and Cock Marsh (Section 10)

Runnymede and Cooper's Hill (Section 12)

Horse Reach, Petersham Meadows and Richmond Hill (Section 14)

Quiet streams and back channels

Opportunities to escape boat traffic and explore off the main river.

All of section 1

Duxford Loop (Section 3)

Swift Ditch (Section 5)

St Patrick's Stream (Section 9)

Hennerton Backwater (Section 9)

Cookham backwaters (Section 11)

Jubilee River (Section 11)

Abbey River (Section 12)

Aits and eyots

Islands to circumnavigate, explore and maybe picnic upon.

Radcot Aits (Section 2)

Medley Eyot and Fiddler's Island (Section 4)

Moulsford Eyots (Section 7)

Cleeve Eyots (Section 7)

Hurley Lock Islands (Section 10)

Desborough Island (Section 13)

Platt's Eyot (Section 13)

Brentford Islands (Section 14)

History and culture

Engaging historical sites which can be appreciated from the water or via forays ashore.

Kelmscott Manor (Section 2)

Godstow Abbey (Section 4)

Mapledurham Mill (Section 8)

River and Rowing Museum (Section 9)

Cliveden House (Section 11)

Windsor Castle and Home Park (Section 12)

All of Section 15

Greenwich (Section 16)

Locks and weir pools

Attractive locks and weirs where you will want to linger. Be extremely careful around the weir pools, however!

Buscot Lock (Section 2)

Iffley Lock (Section 5)

Sandford Pool (Section 5)

Sutton Pools (Section 5)

Day's Lock (Section 6)

Whitchurch Lock (Section 7)

Hambleden Lock (Section 9)

Shepperton Lock (Section 13)

The secluded Upper Thames.

The River Thames

The River Thames is the longest river entirely in England, and has a claim to be the longest in the British Isles (see boxed text, page 53). It measures 347km from its source in the Cotswold Hills to The Nore, a sandbank offshore between Essex and Kent where the North Sea is deemed to begin.

The Thames' name is over 2,000 years old; in 55 BC, invader Julius Caesar learned that it was called *Tamesis*. It derives from either the Celtic *Tems* or the Sanskrit *Tamas*; both words mean 'darkness'. This name was clearly always used for the whole river, but some uninformed Medieval and Tudor writers described the river in two parts, calling it the Isis as far as the River Thame confluence near Dorchester, and the Thamisis (i.e. Thame and Isis combined) below. This misunderstanding has proved persistent, with a stretch in Oxford commonly called 'Isis' and even the Ordnance Survey indecisively labelling the upper river 'Thames or Isis'.

Some facts and figures; the modern river is crossed by 214 bridges and has 17 tunnels beneath it. There are at least 190 islands, around 45 of which are inhabited, with a population of around 3,000 (or 40,000 if you include Canvey Island). The Thames' flow is controlled by 195 weirs around 44 locks through its 105.8m descent to sea level, with another two locks (Richmond and the Thames Barrier) regulating the Tideway flow.

📷 *Middle Thames landscape.*

The character of the River Thames

The river has been divided into four sections in this guidebook, reflecting the differing character of each.

The Upper Thames

"There are dozens of reaches upon the upper Thames with little in sight save the willow, the meadows and a village church tower."

Hilaire Belloc,
The Historic Thames 1907

Despite being over a century old, Belloc's description nicely sums up the upper reaches. Visitors are often amazed to find how quiet and undeveloped the area is. The river rises almost unnoticed in a Cotswold field, fighting a tortuous and often overgrown course to the town of Lechlade, after which there are no riverside villages or towns for over 40km. The young river winds through a landscape of wide flood meadows towards Oxford, whose Osney Bridge has only 2.28m clearance, keeping upstream boat traffic low.

The Middle Thames

Between Oxford and Reading, the Thames is still predominantly a rural river, but is interspersed with attractive and historic small towns and villages. This arguably offers paddlers the best of both worlds. The river traces broad curves through spacious lush meadows, with a fine backdrop of modest wooded hills and chalk downland. It passes between the Berkshire Downs and Chiltern Ridge at Goring Gap, a scenic highlight of the whole river.

The Lower Thames

"Between Reading and London flows the Thames of popular imagination: riverside pubs, rowing clubs, the Henley Regatta and scenes still reminiscent of Jerome K. Jerome's Three Men in a Boat.*"*

Mick Sinclair,

The Thames: A Cultural History 2007

The Lower Thames was historically, and is currently, a landscape of leisure and relaxation. Experiencing this culture from the water has an appeal of its own. From Maidenhead, the broad river's wide plain is increasingly covered with suburban settlement, and fewer of the characteristic meadows survive. Yet, impressively, the Thames remains a green corridor extending right into London.

Aits and eyots

Islands on the Thames are called 'eyots' or 'aits' – both words are pronounced the same, like 'eight'. The words come from the Old English word for an island, *igeth*, which in turn comes from the Indo-European root *akw* meaning 'water' (as in *aqua* etc.).

The Tideway

The Thames becomes tidal at Teddington, yet is still indisputably a river and has over 100km to flow before its end. The Tideway is a landscape of remarkable variety and contrast. The river flows swiftly and powerfully, fuelled by

◻ *The Lower Thames.*

📷 *The busy Tideway.*

a seven-metre tidal range. The approach into Central London is characterised by mansions and landscaped greenery, the so-called 'Arcadian Thames'.

The Thames of Central London is a place of non-stop activity. The river doesn't just flow past the capital's monumental history, it is central to it. Paddling through is an awe-inspiring assault on the senses (over 30 bridges!), the pace only moderating once the Docklands are reached.

Leaving London behind, the shores fall far back as the 'Thames Gateway' is entered, a vast neglected swathe of marshland and old industry. This estuarine region is slated for redevelopment but is currently in a – not unappealing – state of limbo. Where does the river end, and the sea begin? You judge.

📷 *Flood levels, Pinkhill Lock.*

Climate and flows

The Thames drains 12,935 sq km, which includes 38 tributaries and 18 complete river catchments. Leaving Oxford, the end of the Upper Thames, the mean flow is 24.8 cumecs (cubic metres per second) and at Reading, end of the Middle Thames, it is 39.7 cumecs. Teddington Lock is the end of the Lower Thames and start of the Tideway; here the mean flow is 65.8 cumecs, which equates to about 1,250 million gallons a day passing through the weir. In late summer, the flow at Teddington averages 31.6 cumecs. 275 cumecs is considered a spring or winter peak flow; this level was continuously exceeded for a record 52 days in 2014!

The 2014 floods peaked at 524 cumecs, enough to generate *Daily Mail* headlines demanding that Britain's international aid budget be redirected to Berkshire. The river actually flowed higher on seven occasions in the previous century and is believed to have topped 1,000 cumecs in 1894.

The Thames Valley above London is far enough inland to have a 'continental' climate; it enjoys the warmest summer temperatures in the UK, while RAF Benson on the Middle Thames often records England's lowest winter temperatures. Year-round, the urban effect causes London's mean temperature to be 0.5–0.7 °C warmer than elsewhere.

Planning your Journey

"Nothing seems really to matter, that's the charm of it. Whether you get away, or whether you don't; whether you arrive at your destination or whether you reach somewhere else, or whether you never get anywhere at all ..."

The Wind in the Willows, Kenneth Grahame, 1908

Water Rat's advice to Mole sums up the joyful freedom of adventures on the River Thames. However, whether planning for a day trip or a multi-day expedition, selecting the right equipment, checking the river levels and choosing the right challenge for your group will help make your journey an enjoyable and successful experience.

Who?

Most of the Thames is suitable for paddlers of all levels of ability. Complete beginners or novices will find a perfect environment for learning and progressing quickly on the Upper Thames below Lechlade, and the Middle and Lower Thames, provided they plan appropriately. At the other end of the spectrum, the Tideway is only suitable for experienced paddlers with an understanding of the tidal environment.

Canoes or kayaks?

Canoes are open-topped craft within which one or more paddlers sit or kneel, propelling themselves with single-bladed paddles. They are also known as 'open canoes' or 'Canadian canoes'. Kayaks can have closed decks or open decks (known as sit-on-tops or SOTs) but the key difference is that the paddler sits, propelling him or herself with a two-bladed paddle. Some kayaks have seats for more than one paddler. Just to complicate and confuse things, in Britain it is normal to use the word 'canoe' to refer to both canoes and kayaks!

Which is better for the River Thames? Both are great. Canoes carry far more food and equipment, and are quicker to learn how to handle. Kayaks are more manoeuvrable and less affected by wind. The Port of London Authority (PLA) advises that the Tideway with its waves and currents is "more suited to kayaks with enclosed cockpits". Specialised sea kayaks are recommended, although open canoes have made the journey, with great care.

Other kinds of paddlecraft are of course available. Inflatable kayaks are now common, a hybrid of raft and kayak. They are easy to transport off the water (onto trains and so forth) but slow and susceptible to the wind. The PLA does not consider them suitable for the Tideway below Putney Bridge. Stand up paddleboards (SUPs) are hugely popular, and are being increasingly used for longer trips. Current designs don't leave much option for carrying gear! Paddleboards are restricted on the Tideway from Putney Bridge down (see table).

The Thames Skills and Knowledge (TSK) qualifications for paddleboarders were introduced in 2015, and are compulsory for paddling below Putney Bridge; Level 1 for group members, Level 2 for group leaders. Further details from www.boatingonthethames.co.uk. The author and his friends have journeyed on the Thames using open canoes, racing canoes, paddleboards, touring kayaks, sea kayaks, racing kayaks, rafts and surf skis. In 2016, a group of Scout leaders descended the river on a swan-shaped pedalo! The Thames is also popular with wild swimmers (the author experienced no ill effects from his morning and evening swims during book research), although swimming is banned on the Tideway. The following books are recommended if you want to learn more about selecting and handling paddlecraft:

British Canoe Union *Canoe and Kayak Handbook*, Franco Ferrero (ed.), Pesda Press, 2002, ISBN 9780953195657

Canoeing, Ray Goodwin, Pesda Press, 2016, ISBN 9781906095543

Sit-on-top Kayak, Derek Hairon, Pesda Press, 2007, ISBN 9781906095024

Above Putney Pier	Beginners recommended to be accompanied by a TSK qualified paddler. No paddleboards after dark without TSK qualifications.
Below Putney Pier	No paddleboards from three hours before to one hour after HW London Bridge. Must carry VHF. Must possess appropriate TSK qualifications.
Chelsea Bridge to Tower Bridge	No paddleboards from 1100 to 1800 between Good Friday and 30th September. Must possess appropriate TSK qualifications.
Below Chelsea Bridge	No paddleboards after dark or solo.
Below Tower Bridge	No paddleboards.

Canoe hire

Carrying gear

The canoe hire industry is growing along the Thames, with many companies offering equipment hire, guiding and coaching. Usually they also provide river advice and some offer a shuttle service to return you to the start of your trip.

Whether you are travelling for a day or a week, your equipment will need protecting and waterproofing. Hire companies sometimes loan watertight plastic barrels for use in canoes, which helpfully keep large amounts of gear dry and protected from knocks. It is

Advice from a hire company

There are a growing number of canoe hire and guiding companies along the Thames where you can hire canoes, kayaks or double kayaks for anything from a few hours to a multi-day paddling trip.

Discuss your group and your requirements with them. You should reasonably expect a map, a safety talk and some guidance on paddling before you venture forth. If you are a novice and in doubt about your capabilities, we recommend that you ask for a guide to accompany you, especially if there are children involved. If you have children in your group, it's a good idea to have paddled the section previously or have had previous paddling experience. Many operators allow you to paddle downstream and will come to collect you and your canoe at journey's end. Many routes are serviced by public transport which can be coordinated to get you back to either your car or home.

For most of the year the Thames is flowing at a great level for beginners' canoeing but should always be avoided when the water

levels are high or notably rising. If there has been persistent heavy rain before your trip, you should call the hire company for advice, and also check the Environment Agency's River Thames Conditions website: riverconditions.environment-agency.gov.uk. The Environment Agency operates a 'strong stream' warning system on the non-tidal Thames. Hire companies should not operate during red 'strong stream' conditions or yellow 'stream increasing/decreasing' conditions. Green is good to go.

Take sensible clothing, food and drink [see this book for advice]. Paddling the Thames is a lovely way to enjoy the company of friends and family. Take your time and relish the journey, surroundings and wildlife instead of trying to break records. No matter how familiar you think you are with the river, you'll find that paddling it is a special experience which allows you to appreciate it at its absolute best.

Andrew Jackson, Thames Canoes, Marlow

www.thamescanoes.com

PLANNING YOUR JOURNEY

📷 *Waterproof barrels and dry bags.*

recommended to tie them securely into the canoe, however! The barrels are too large for kayaks, so the best option for these is to use small and flexible 'dry bags' which are sealed by a roll-top closure. These fit down the back of most kayaks, with a little persuasion. Unless you buy very expensive designs, dry bags are still likely to leak; consider putting your kit in thick plastic bags inside the dry bags. Camera equipment and other fragile expensive equipment should ideally be protected in solid cases with padding, such as those produced by Peli Products. Barrels, dry bags and solid cases will still result in soaking or destroyed kit if you forget to close and seal them properly.

Safety

"A revolver and one or two good dogs should I think be always taken as precautions on these camping expeditions."

George D Leslie, *Our River* 1888

This section is about *safety*; selecting appropriate equipment and understanding hazards encountered on the Thames, to avoid getting into difficulty.

In normal summer water levels, the River Thames is a forgiving and safe environment which is entirely suited to novices and the inexperienced, if a little common sense is applied in planning, selecting equipment and avoiding hazards. There are important exceptions to this rule, however:

- A high water level exacerbates all normal hazards, making them harder to avoid and more dangerous. We don't recommend recreational paddling on the Thames when it is on yellow or red strong stream conditions (see below).
- The Tideway below Teddington Lock is a markedly different environment with some significant hazards. Only venture here if you are experienced in tidal waters.

Paddlers who want to learn more about the subject of safety (and rescue) are recommended to seek specialist training, or to consult *White Water Safety and Rescue* by Franco Ferrero, Pesda Press, 2006, ISBN 9780954706159.

Clothing and equipment
Flotation

Whichever craft you float down the Thames in, it must have some form of fixed buoyancy to prevent it from sinking when waterlogged. This is usually achieved through inflatable air bags, solid foam or sealed chambers in the boat.

Entrapment hazards

Make sure that any ropes, straps or suchlike are securely stowed away and cannot form a loop or point of entrapment/snagging for a paddler's foot or hand.

📷 *Marsh Weir in high water.*

Buoyancy aids

A well-fitted buoyancy aid is essential, and will make a swim much less dangerous.

Clothing

Your clothing needs to protect you from becoming hypothermic by remaining warm when wet and by providing a shield from the wind. Wetsuits do this well, but will probably be over-warm and restrictive in summer. An ideal solution might be to wear polypropylene or fleece thermals with a cagoule on top. Legs need similar protection, and don't forget a warm hat for your head! Helmets also retain heat well, and may be a good idea for young or inexperienced paddlers. Footwear should offer protection when scrambling ashore on muddy banks. You should also carry spare dry clothing.

Sun protection

Waterproof sun cream and a brimmed hat will protect your skin and save you from the prospect of having to paddle with painful, chafing sunburn on the following day.

Phones

A mobile phone (packed in a waterproof container) is worth carrying. It can be used for summoning assistance in an emergency or to let people know if you are going to be a bit late so that they don't worry.

River hazards

Weirs

The Thames' locks each have at least one artificial weir, where water either falls over a sill, or rushes through an open sluice.

They have buoyed chains or similar barriers upstream of them (although there are exceptions, such as Richmond Lock), and these give you plenty of space to avoid them and find a safe channel. However, this can be a different story at high levels.

You are not permitted to 'run' the weirs; none are built with paddler safety or enjoyment in mind, and many are lethal. Weirs contain all manner of user-unfriendly metalwork. Worse, the falling water loses energy by forming 'stoppers'; waves which fold back on themselves below drops, 'stopping' or even holding and drowning paddlers.

The pools below weirs form some of the most beautiful spots on the river. Explore these in low water levels only, approaching from downstream, keeping a long way clear of the area affected by the weir current. The white-water below certain weirs is carefully used for play by expert paddlers, in very specific conditions; see *English White Water*, Pesda Press, 2014, ISBN 9781906095451 for details. Everyone else ... should steer well clear.

Obstacles

Be careful approaching bridges, as the current piles onto the upstream side of the bridge pillars. Some are designed to smoothly redirect water (and paddlers?), but regardless, steer well clear. Tree branches and other junk sometimes pile onto the pillars, causing a significant hazard.

Moored boats, buoys and other fixed floating objects can be dangerous in high water. The current flows swiftly towards and under these things, with no cushion wave to push paddlers to safety – avoid! On the Tideway's fast currents, the pontoons and giant metal buoys are a major hazard.

Tree branches and bushes lurk in the water along the riverbanks. Usually these 'strainers' are simple to avoid; however rivers flow towards the outsides of bends and erode back the banks, so in high water you can find yourself being drawn towards or beneath overhanging foliage; steer to avoid. Occasionally, whole trees fall into the river, forming natural sieves; totally avoid!

Below Mapledurham Weir.

Low branches on the Upper Thames.

Other river users at Marlow.

Other river users

"Steam launches are too often the curse of the river. Driving along at an excessive rate of speed, with an utter disregard to punts and rowing boats which are left floundering helplessly in their wash."   Charles Dickens,
Dictionary of the Thames 1887

The steam launches are nowadays replaced by pleasure cruisers, whose owners' inclination to respect the 8kph speed limit is often inversely proportional to the size of their craft. The idiots who give cruiser owners a bad name are perhaps more hazardous to the riverbanks and their wildlife than you, but stay alert nonetheless. Turn your boat to face large wash and paddle straight over it; this advice is especially pertinent on the Tideway where the traffic can exceed 30 knots/56kph!

On most stretches of the river, traffic is light; you'll generally meet several boats at a lock, and then see nothing for a long while after. Rowing eights travel at up to 15 knots/28kph, have their backs to you, and are pointy at the ends. Keep well clear of their path. If there is a risk of collision, shout out a warning or blow a whistle.

Seeking help

If you find yourself in serious difficulty and in need of assistance, do not hesitate to call the UK emergency phone number **999**. Give details of your group, your difficulty and perhaps most importantly, your location. The operator will summon the Police, Ambulance, Fire Service, Lowland Rescue, Coastguard or Lifeboat as appropriate.

The Thames is paddleable year-round, although the section above Lechlade can become shallow in late summer.

To ascertain the level of the non-tidal Thames before setting off to paddle, you have two options;

- Visit the Environment Agency (EA) website riverconditions. environment-agency.gov.uk
- Call the Environment Agency Floodline on 0845 988 1188 to hear recorded information and advice (select option 1 and when prompted, dial 011131).

The website gives readouts from numerous gauging stations along the Thames and its tributaries. However, looking at their graphs, you'll realise that the data is actually of limited use. The system is set up to warn of floods, and little else; major changes are needed in the river's flow before the graphs noticeably alter. Strong stream conditions (not the same as high water conditions) are clearly flagged up at lock gates, by displaying coloured boards:

- Red boards mean that the stream is so strong that the EA advise all boats not to navigate.
- Yellow boards are usually accompanied by the self-explanatory text: 'Caution stream increasing' or 'Caution stream decreasing', and mean that they advise unpowered boats not to navigate, i.e. you.

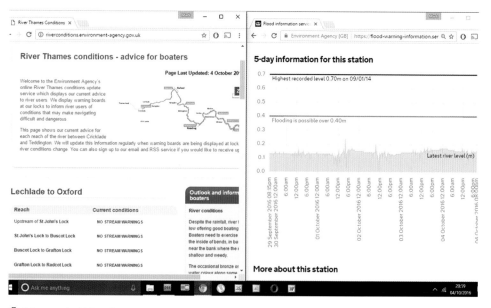

Online water level information.

📷 *Channel marker.*

These are simple for the non-tidal river:

- The speed limit above
  Teddington Lock is 8kph.
- Stay right of oncoming boats, where
  it is safe and practical to do so.
- Give way to boats coming downstream at constrictions, bridges,
  sharp bends and so forth.

*"Locks are generally good places to idle at; the
great lever handles are very convenient to lounge
on, the keepers have mostly something interesting to tell you, while the excitement of passing
boats never fails in its variety."*

George D Leslie, *Our River* 1888

Negotiating locks is a pleasant aspect of
paddling the Thames. Racing paddlers
shoulder their boats and run around them,
but paddling through the locks is much more
relaxing and enjoyable.

There are 45 locks in total (not including
Blake's Lock, on the River Kennet but administered as a Thames lock). Those from King's

upstream are manually operated, while the
remainder are hydraulically powered. All are
manned by lock keepers (assisted by volunteers in the summer), but they can also be
operated 'self service' out of hours and during
their keeper's lunch breaks. The exceptions
are the final two (tidal) locks; Teddington and
Richmond are both manned 24 hours and only
operated by keepers. Richmond is the only
lock belonging to the PLA, while all others are
in the care of the Environment Agency.

All locks can be portaged; most have steps to
leave the water on the lock's upstream side,
and jetties downstream to launch from. Portaging locks can be awkward with a heavy boat. A
few locks have 'rollers' at water level allowing
you to drag your boat across the lock island,
otherwise most touring paddlers will choose

📷 *Hand-operated lock.*

📷 Lock keeper at Shifford.

to pass through the lock. If the lock gates are closed when you arrive and there are no other craft waiting outside, you may have to wave a paddle or shout to attract the keeper's attention. Once the gates are open, follow the keeper's instructions; you'll usually be asked to paddle to the front of the lock and hold onto the hanging chains while the water level drops. The further downstream you are, the more likely it is that you'll share the lock with

📷 Lock sign.

larger craft; not a problem, as the lock keeper will give clear directions to all. When the water has lowered and the gates open, remember to shout your thanks as you paddle out!

The manual locks on the Upper Thames are fun to operate. Each gate has a big wheel and two coloured posts, indicating open (red) or closed (white). Simply turn the wheel to open or close the sluices on that gate. Make sure that you close the sluices on the downstream gates **before** opening the sluices on the upstream gates, unless you wish to drain the river! When you have passed through a lock, leave the lock empty and the sluices on the downstream gates open.

Locks usually have basic facilities such as taps for drinking water, and toilets. A number permit camping, for those walking or boating along the river.

No.	Lock	Drop	Grid reference	Distance from previous lock	Distance from source of Thames	Rollers?	Camping?
Upper Thames							
1	St John's	0.85m	SU 222 990	0km	38.3km		
2	Buscot	1.69m	SU 230 981	1.7km	40km		
3	Grafton	1.11m	SU 271 992	5.4km	45.4km		
4	Radcot	1.48m	SU 296 002	3.5km	48.9km		
5	Rushey	1.82m	SP 323 001	3.6km	52.5km		Y
6	Shifford	2.23m	SP 370 011	6.7km	59.2km		Y
7	Northmoor	1.24m	SP 431 021	7.6km	66.8km		
8	Pinkhill	1.05m	SP 441 071	6.4km	73.2km		Y
9	Eynsham	0.84m	SP 445 086	2.2km	75.4km		Y
10	King's	0.77m	SP 479 103	4.3km	79.7km		Y
11	Godstow	1.57m	SP 485 089	1.8km	81.5km		
12	Osney	1.89m	SP 504 059	4km	85.5km		
Middle Thames							
13	Iffley	0.81m	SP 526 037	3.6km	89.1km	Y	
14	Sandford	2.69m	SP 531 013	2.7km	91.8km		
15	Abingdon	1.89m	SU 507 971	7.5km	99.3km		
16	Culham	2.41m	SU 508 949	4.1km	103.4km		
17	Clifton	1.03m	SU 547 947	5.3km	108.7km		
18	Day's	1.58m	SU 569 936	4.2km	112.9km		Y
19	Benson	1.87m	SU 613 913	6.3km	119.2km		
20	Cleeve	0.89m	SU 601 818	10.6km	129.8km		
21	Goring	1.77m	SU 597 809	1km	130.8km		
22	Whitchurch	1.01m	SU 634 768	6.6km	137.4km		
23	Mapledurham	2.05m	SU 668 768	3.8km	141.2km		
24	Caversham	1.44m	SU 721 740	7km	148.2km		

No.	Lock	Drop	Grid reference	Distance from previous lock	Distance from source of Thames	Rollers?	Camping?
Lower Thames							
25	Sonning	1.63m	SU 252 754	4.2km	152.4km		
26	Shiplake	1.55m	SU 776 787	4.5km	156.9km		
27	Marsh	1.33m	SU 774 817	4.3km	161.2km		
28	Hambleden	1.44m	SU 782 852	5.3km	166.5km		
29	Hurley	1.05m	SU 827 843	5.8km	172.3km		Y
30	Temple	1.23m	SU 837 844	1km	173.3km		
31	Marlow	2.16m	SU 854 861	2.7km	176km		
32	Cookham	1.3m	SU 906 855	6.9km	182.9km		Y
33	Boulter's	2.39m	SU 903 824	3.3km	186.2km		
34	Bray	1.46m	SU 910 798	3.6km	189.8km		
35	Boveney	1.47m	SU 945 778	5.1km	194.9km	Y	
36	Romney	2.01m	SU 970 779	3.7km	198.6km		
37	Old Windsor	1.74m	SU 995 748	4.9km	203.5km		
38	Bell Weir	1.82m	TQ 017 721	4.7km	208.2km		
39	Penton Hook	1.22m	TQ 044 695	4.6km	212.8km		
40	Chertsey	1.22m	TQ 054 668	3.1km	215.9km		
41	Shepperton	2.03m	TQ 073 659	3.3km	219.2km		
42	Sunbury	1.87m	TQ 110 685	4.9km	224.1km	Y	
43	Molesey	1.87m	TQ 151 686	4.7km	228.8km	Y	
44	Teddington	2.68m	TQ 166 716	7.8km	236.6km	Y	
The Tideway							
45	Richmond	2m	TQ 170 751	5.2km	241.8km	Y	

The Thames offers 217km of paddling above Teddington Lock, before we start measuring back channels! Below Teddington, the Tideway offers another potential 110km+. This book's guides to sections of the Thames are of course paddling trip itineraries, each taking from half a day to a day to complete. Assume that you will cover from three to six kilometres an hour, depending upon your craft and experience. Numerous launch points have been suggested, allowing you to tailor your own itinerary. An A to B trip will require you to shuttle vehicles or use public transport to get back to the start after paddling. One way to avoid this is an 'out and back' paddle; there are numerous parts of the Thames where it is possible to return on different channels. Further trip planning ideas are given in the 'Variations' notes accompanying some sections.

How about if you want to paddle for longer than just one day? Suggested below is an itinerary for a multi-day expedition. The daily distances are inconsistent, but reflect the limited campsites available. The itinerary finishes at the first big car park on the Tideway; any expedition continuing through London would have to arrange bed and breakfast or hotel accommodation along the riverside, or arrange pick-ups from a support crew.

It possibly goes without saying, but for the removal of any doubt ... should you have the opportunity to descend the whole river from the Cotswolds to London, then *do it*! This is a truly remarkable journey, one that will engage, challenge and inspire. If you have the skills and experience, we also recommend continuing through the Tideway. The feeling of accomplishment at paddling under Tower Bridge, having started out on a Gloucestershire stream, is indescribable.

Day	From	To	Distance	Distance from source
1 Walk!	Source	Cricklade	19.7km	19.7km
2	Cricklade	Lechlade	18.8km	38.4km
3	Lechlade	Pinkhill Lock	34.8km	73.2km
4	Pinkhill Lock	Clifton Hampden	35.5km	108.7km
5	Clifton Hampden	Mapledurham Lock	32.5km	141.2km
6	Mapledurham Lock	Hurley Lock	31.1km	172.3km
7	Hurley Lock	Bray Lock	17.5km	189.8km
8	Bray Lock	Chertsey Lock	26.1km	215.9km
9	Chertsey Lock	Richmond (Ham Street)	23.1km	239km

PLANNING YOUR JOURNEY

Ian's expeditions

I've completed four Thames trips over 200 kilometres long. I first got the idea in 1994, when walking the beautiful Ridgeway National Trail near Goring. Walking the Thames river bank, I felt as if at any moment I might catch a glimpse of Toad of Toad Hall erratically sculling up the river; I was hooked. When researching the trip I was amazed to discover that the Thames started near Swindon!

I love travelling under my own steam on unsupported adventures. The Thames has allowed me to indulge this passion twice by kayak and twice by open canoe. On the first trip I completed the trip in a kayak bought for seven pounds which had been resting in a tree for five years prior to me buying it! Travelling in this kayak from Cricklade to North London (via Brentford Lock) was an incredible experience. Launching in a rural location in the middle of the countryside, travelling by river and ending the journey a week later in a busy capital city has to be experienced. It is just so different from any other means of travel.

The river allows those with little paddling experience access to a long river journey. This has allowed me to share my passion fully with others. The Thames is diverse in its attractions, so there is always something of interest for most people just around the next bend.

It is never too long before tired arms can have a rest, waiting for the usually cheerful lock keepers. The locks are also a good opportunity for a chat and a joke with fellow river users. On my last trip I was supplied with a small buffet and a very pleasing glass of red from a cruiser while waiting for a lock near Henley.

 Ian at Temple Lock.

📷 *Ian at Temple Weir.*

There are countless opportunities to observe nature in all its glory. I have seen over one hundred swans at one time, from a single vantage point. Beware; the higher up the Thames, the more aggressive they tend to be in spring. As you travel down-river however, they only seem to be interested in food. You are guaranteed to see geese aplenty, often noisily chaperoning their young around the riverbanks. Then of course, there is the daily kingfisher count, always a thrill. For much of the journey there are the slowly circling red kites and sometimes the glimpse of sparrowhawk or kestrel. Once I even saw a roe deer swim across the river. Then there are the birds far from the sea which they are more usually associated with; the cormorants and the terns, the latter elegantly dipping their beaks while skimming the water.

Old Father Thames winds its way through quintessentially beautiful English land-scape. Never far from built-up areas, yet never does the non-tidal Thames feel over-whelmed by man's interference in the way roads so often do. Even travelling through a city, the banks of the Thames mostly make you feel you are in a remote rural area.

Most of the river must look much the same as it did in Jerome K Jerome's time. This is further enhanced by so many historic boats being beautifully maintained and visible on the river. The classic 'slipper launch' always makes me smile whenever I see one, with its polished chrome and elegant lacquered stern sweeping down to the water. Like so much you see as you paddle, a reminder of a bygone age, with traditions valued and maintained in all their perfection.

Ian Holmes

The Duke of Edinburgh's Awards for 14–24 year olds are intended to "inspire, guide and support young people in their self-development". A key component of the awards is "To inspire young people to develop initiative and a spirit of adventure and discovery, by planning, training for and completing an adventurous self-sufficient journey, as part of a team."

The Upper, Middle and Lower Thames see use by DofE expedition groups for expedition training or for final qualifying expeditions. The river suits this for a range of reasons; the

Award	Recommended environment	Duration of expedition	Advised distances
Bronze	Canals, rivers or other inland waterways and lakes. The water and area may be familiar to participants.	2 days, 1 night, 6 hours of planned activity daily	16–20km daily, 32–40km total
Silver	Canals, rivers or other inland waterways and lakes in rural areas. The water must be unfamiliar to the participants and present an appropriate challenge. There is an expectation that the conditions will be related to the age and experience of the participants and represent a progression between Bronze and Gold.	3 days, 2 nights, 7 hours of planned activity daily	22km daily, 65km total
Gold	Rivers or other inland waterways and lakes in rural areas, sheltered coastal waters or estuaries. The water must be unfamiliar to the participants and must present an appropriate challenge. At Gold level routes should be in or pass through wild country. Moving water, either by current or tide, or large bodies of water, should be sought where possible.	4 days, 3 nights, 8 hours of planned activity daily	32km daily, 128km total

Upper and Middle Thames flow through areas fitting the DofE's definitions of 'rural', there is an undisputed right of navigation, riverside campsites are available at intervals, equipment and guides/instructors are available to hire, and it is easy for a DofE supervisor to monitor a group's progress from bridges, locks and the Thames Path.

The award criteria above are met by different sections of the Thames, although the Tideway can't be recommended without some very specialist training. An expedition might begin by negotiating the uppermost sections of the Thames and could continue as far as Reading.

The Thames has excellent potential for selecting engaging and challenging expedition aims; the wildlife and environment are easy to access and observe, while the region's history and culture offer more ideas. Why not investigate the GHQ Stop Line, or the volume of traffic at locks, or the impact of past floods, for example?

Further advice on DofE expeditions over water can also be found in Chapter 13 of the *Expedition Guide*:

The Duke of Edinburgh's Award Expedition Guide, Alex Davies, The Award Scheme Ltd., 2012, ISBN 9780905425207

Quotes from boys of Abingdon School, Oxfordshire

"It was great to see the amount of wildlife on the Thames; we were often amazed by the Canada geese flying overhead in formation, the red kite circling the river banks or kingfisher perched on a branch."

"The lock keepers were so friendly throughout the trip, taking time to talk to us and give us encouragement."

"Navigating the rowers beside the university was interesting, but great to see them training from water level."

"We spent four long days paddling the Thames from Castle Eaton to Reading – it was a massive challenge but the long distances certainly prepared us for our assessment."

"I loved the remoteness of the River Thames. I always thought of the Thames as the river through London. I never knew it was so quiet and peaceful."

"The first day of our Silver practice was a breeze compared to day two from Lechlade to Bablock Hythe: the early morning fog meant we couldn't see a thing and had to paddle so close together that we kept crashing into each other!"

"Having paddled numerous rivers as part of my three DofE awards, I can honestly say that I found the Thames the nicest; the constantly changing environment from countryside to urban industry meant every corner was something different."

Which bank?

Throughout this book, the terms 'river left' and 'river right' are commonly used to locate features. 'River left' is simply the left hand bank when you are looking downriver, and 'river right' is ... okay, you get it.

📷 *Thames Path signage.*

Thames Paths

Thames Path National Trail follows the river for 184 miles (296km) from the source to the Thames Barrier. It is signposted along the riverbank for the vast majority of its length, with paths on both banks through central London. Below Gravesend, the Saxon Shore Way continues east along the Kent coast while opposite, the Thames Estuary Path winds along the Essex marshes. A grand single estuary path is currently being linked up along both shores. These paths are worth being aware of as they offer public waterside access and the possibility of riverside walking shuttles.

Thames Path in the Country, David Sharp, Aurum Press, 2016, ISBN 9781781315750

The Thames Path in London, Phoebe Clapham, Aurum Press, 2016, ISBN 9781781315743

📷 *The source.*

Section	1:50000 Landranger map(s)	1:25000 Explorer map(s)
Source	163	168, 169
1	163	169, 170
2	163, 164	170, 180
3	164	180
4	164	180
5	164	170, 180
6	164, 174	170
7	164, 175	159, 170, 171
8	175	159, 170, 171
9	175	159, 171
10	175	171, 172
11	175	160, 172
12	175, 176	160
13	176	160, 161
14	176	161, 173
15	176, 177	161, 173
16	177	161, 162
17	177	162, 163
18	177, 178	149, 163, 176

© Approaching Blackfriars Bridge.

Paddling the Tideway

"I walk my beat before London Town,
Five hours up and seven down.
Up I go till I end my run
At Tide-end-town, which is Teddington."

The River's Tale, Rudyard Kipling, 1911

The Thames Tideway offers challenges and rewards quite unlike any other paddling trip in Britain. The factors involved in planning and enjoying a safe trip may seem daunting, however do not be put off! Trust us on this one – you want to paddle the Tideway.

Tides

As the poem suggests, the tide floods up-stream for about five hours, and ebbs down-stream for around seven hours. The tide range can be as much as seven metres and flows of over four knots (7.4kph) are common along narrow and channelled stretches. These powerful flows can generate standing waves under bridges, and exaggerate the steepness of the wash from boats travelling against the flow. The relentless current could potentially drag paddlers into and under fixed obstacles in their path; buoys, pontoons, ships! You need to be alert for such hazards at all times. At high tide, the river is often hemmed in by un-assailable artificial banks, while the beaches exposed at low tide can be inaccessible due to soft mud (especially those downstream of the Thames Barrier).

On rare occasions when the Thames Barrier is closed, there will be no tidal flow and confused conditions in general.

Plan your journey to travel with the tide flow, unless you are looking to prove some macho/masochistic point.

Difference in hours and minutes from London Bridge (at Tower Pier)	For HW...	For LW...
Teddington Lock	add 1 01	XXX
Richmond Lock	add 1 01	add 2 50
Kew Bridge	add 0 52	add 2 46
Barnes Railway Bridge	add 0 44	add 2 19
Hammersmith Bridge	add 0 38	add 1 58
Putney Bridge	add 0 31	add 1 38
Chelsea Bridge	add 0 14	add 0 45
Westminster Bridge	add 0 10	add 0 30
Greenland Dock Entrance	sub 0 9	sub 0 14

The tidal foreshore at Putney.

Tideway flows

As well as the tidal flows, fluvial (i.e. river) flows still of course have an effect. After the floods of 2014, the PLA introduced a 'Flag' system for flows (see table opposite).

"The 'Ebb Tide Flag Warning' system alerts rowers, canoeists, and other small recreational vessels of conditions on the river. This system is mainly for when the ebb tide and fluvial flows combine to make river conditions very perilous."

The flag warnings are regularly updated and can be found at www.pla.co.uk and www.boatingonthethames.co.uk.

Traffic

Traffic is much bigger, faster and more frequent than on the non-tidal river; below Putney, it is Britain's busiest waterway. Because most traffic will be faster than you, always keep a good lookout behind. Keeping your group close together will make it easier for others to monitor your movements.

If a vessel gives five short blasts, it is warning you to **"Look out"**. One long blast means that a boat is about to leave a pier, not a time to attempt passing!

The traffic is busiest in Central London at weekends, therefore the PLA strongly encourages paddlers to pass through before 10.00 am.

Speed limits

While you are unlikely to challenge the limits below using paddle power, they will give a clue as to the traffic hazard you'll face.

RED FLAG	Extreme Caution – EBB TIDE Very Strong Fluvial Flows	Fluvial flows are very strong. Conditions are difficult and dangerous. All man-powered vessels are advised not to go afloat on the ebb tide.
YELLOW FLAG	Caution – EBB TIDE Strong Fluvial Flows	All river users of man-powered vessels should navigate with extreme caution and consider whether it is safe for them to go afloat on the ebb tide.
GREEN FLAG	Average Fluvial Flows	All river users to navigate with caution and maintain a proper lookout.
BLACK FLAG	Caution – Low Fluvial Flows	Tidal flow is lower than usual. River users should expect lower than predicted tides especially around low water.

- Teddington to Wandsworth Bridge (first road bridge after Putney Bridge) – 8 knots/approx. 15kph. Rowing boats and their escort craft are exempt from these limits.
- Wandsworth Bridge to Margaretness (bend of the river after Woolwich) – 12 knots/approx. 22kph.
- There are two High Speed Zones where exempted craft (notably Thames Clippers and similar passenger cruisers) are allowed to go faster. These vessels have a flashing yellow light on top.

1. Wandsworth Bridge to Lambeth Bridge – 25 knots/approx. 46kph.
2. St Saviour's Dock (just below Tower Bridge) to Margaretness – 30 knots/approx. 56kph(!)

- Police and other emergency services are exempt from all limits on the Tideway.
- Below Margaretness – no limits, large ships are 'advised' to keep to 10 knots/18kph past Gravesend.

The traffic increases in size through the Tideway ...

Battersea Railway Bridge – note bridge lights.

These must be familiar to all in your group.

- Keep looking around at all times.
- Stay well clear of, and give way to, larger craft.
- Keep to the right-hand (starboard) side at all times (i.e. the right-hand side looking ahead, whether heading upriver or downriver). Note that the flow pushes towards the outside of bends; but still keep right.
- Keep out of the Fairway, where possible. This is the central deep channel, for larger vessels.
- In High Speed Zones – keep as far right as possible!
- Pass pontoons, piers, moored boats and suchlike on the inside (along the bank), as long as you judge it practical and safe to do so. Exceptions to this rule are Embankment Pier (not permitted) and Waterloo Pier (not possible).
- Only cross the river when you are sure that you will not get in anyone's path. Keep a good lookout and cross in a tight group, not in single file.
- Between Teddington and Putney Bridge, rowers have right of way along the sides, and the centre of the river (Fairway) is for other vessels. However, paddlers can usually still squeeze along the shore.
- Between Syon Reach and Putney only, paddlers are obliged to 'work the slacks' if they are paddling *against* the tidal stream. This means that they have to cross to the inside of bends (where the current is slower) and stay close inshore. The Crossing Zones are marked by red and green buoys.
- Downstream of the Thames Barrier avoid the buoyed channels, which are not always central to the river but follow the deeper water (for the needs of very large vessels, which you won't want to get near!).

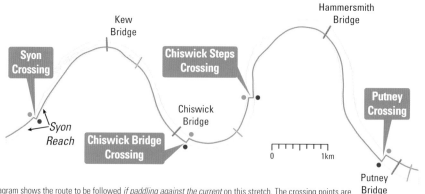

This diagram shows the route to be followed *if paddling against the current* on this stretch. The crossing points are marked on the water by green buoys (on the north side of the river) and red buoys (on the south side of the river).

⌖ *Working the slacks between Syon Reach and Putney Bridge.*

📷 *Richmond Half-Tide Lock.*

Bridges

Bridges display coloured lights or discs above arches indicating where you should pass beneath. Use the bridge arch closest to the shore, unless it is closed. Abide by these safety directions and be aware that cameras monitor the arches:

- Three red lights/discs
  – archway closed
- Two orange lights/discs – navigation (Fairway) arch – archway open
- One white light/bale of straw – archway open but height restricted
- White flashing – large vessel in the vicinity (very quick flash means two or more) – keep away!

Richmond Lock

Richmond half-tide lock is a mechanical weir used to maintain at least 1.72 metres depth of water upstream. When the downstream water level ebbs down to half-tide, the weir is lowered into place and paddlers have to portage using the muddy slipway under the river left arch; note that powerful boils can materialise downstream. The weir is (impressively) lifted out of the water for around two hours either side of high water. With the weir lifted out, you can paddle straight through on flat water. It is possible to contact the lock keeper on VHF Channel 80.

The 'draw-off' is when the weir is left raised for about a month annually, while maintenance takes place. This is usually between October and December.

The Thames Barrier

The Barrier displays lights indicating the channel to paddle through; green arrows indicate which channel to take, three red lights mean a channel is closed.

If you are carrying VHF or phone, you are obliged to call London VTS (Vehicle Traffic Service) on Channel 14 (see Communication below for phone numbers) to ask for permission to pass through the Barrier. Call when you enter the Thames Barrier Control Zone, which reaches from Blackwall Point to Margaretness. If you aren't carrying either (not recommended), then pass through the channel indicated by the green arrows but stay alert for other traffic.

Notices to Mariners

The PLA asks paddlers to check and keep abreast of the latest Notices to Mariners, which can be found at www.pla.co.uk/Safety. They are updated frequently and advise of arch closures, building works, events taking place and so forth.

Night paddling

Night paddling on the Tideway is definitely only for those with considerable expertise and local experience. London VTS must always be informed of paddlers in the dark below Putney Bridge.

Apart from the fact that it is of course dark, the cruiser traffic is much faster. The PLA states "lights must be displayed at all times of restricted visibility", and specifies that a

📷 *Thames Barrier.*

constant diffused white light should be fixed to both the bow and the stern, visible through 180 degrees and from 800m distance. This could be achieved with torches taped to the deck and diffused through plastic milk bottles. Reflective/hi-vis clothing should be worn, also consider using reflective tape, head torches, LED sticks and so forth to increase visibility. All lights must be white. Avoid dazzling other river users.

Communication

Paddlers are advised to inform London VTS of paddling plans before setting out, and after safe return. For Central London, paddlers are **strongly advised**, and for Westminster Bridge to Tower Bridge, they are **obliged**. They can be contacted by VHF or phone.

London VTS strongly advises paddlers to carry VHF; paddleboards **must** carry them below Putney Bridge. London VTS maintains a continuous listening watch on the channels outlined below. Sea kayakers familiar with using VHF on the coast may be surprised by the sheer volume of radio traffic! If you do not have VHF, a waterproofed phone should be carried.

Area	VHF Channel	Phone number	Navigational broadcasts on VHF
Teddington to Crayfordness	14	020 8855 0315	15 minutes and 45 minutes past each hour
Crayfordness to Sea Reach No. 4 Buoy	68	01747 562215	On and at 30 minutes past each hour
Sea Reach No. 4 Buoy to the seaward limit	69	01747 562215	15 minutes and 45 minutes past each hour

Tideway emergencies

Seek assistance in one of these ways:

- A MAYDAY call by VHF on Channel 16 or the current London VTS channel
- A distress alert on VHF DSC
- Dialling 999 or 112 and asking for the Coastguard

London Coastguard is responsible for coordinating search and rescue activity as far as Canvey Island (beyond is Thames Coastguard). Assistance to paddlers would most likely arrive in the form of an RNLI lifeboat. RNLI lifeboats are stationed at Teddington, Chiswick, Waterloo Pier (Tower), Gravesend, Southend-on-Sea and Sheerness. Tower and Chiswick regularly top the league tables as the UK's busiest stations! Tower launched 543 times in 2014.

Further information

The Port of London Authority publishes outstanding resources for paddlers. Their *Recreational Users Guide* is a map of the Tideway, downloadable from their website and also available on water-resistant paper. They also supply *Paddling on the Tideway*, a detailed Code of Conduct for paddlers. Sign up to the Tidal Thames Navigators' Club to get free copies of these and other useful bumf, as well as receiving emailed Notices to Mariners.

www.pla.co.uk – the Port of London Authority

www.boatingonthethames.co.uk – the PLA's website for recreational boaters

www.youtube.com/user/portoflondon – the PLA's excellent YouTube channel

Lifeboat.

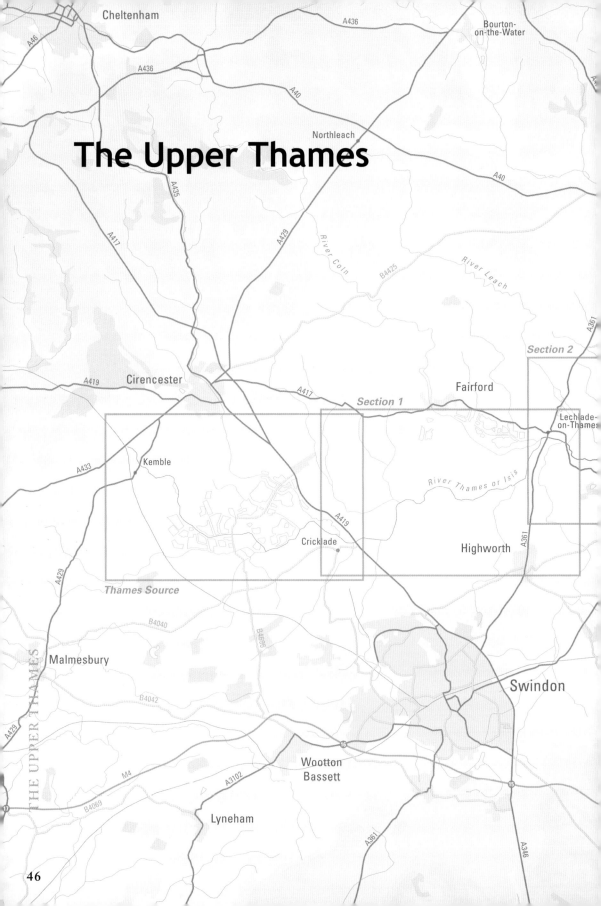

The Upper Thames

Cheltenham

Bourton-on-the-Water

Northleach

River Coln

River Leach

B4425

Cirencester

Section 2

Fairford

Section 1

Lechlade-on-Thames

Kemble

River Thames or Isis

Cricklade

Highworth

Thames Source

B4040

Malmesbury

Swindon

Wootton Bassett

Lyneham

THE UPPER THAMES

Charlbury

River Evenlode

A4095

A44

A4095

Kidlington

A4260

A44

B4027

River Windrush

Witney

A40

Carterton

Section 4

Eynsham

A40

B4449

Oxford

A40

A34

A40

Section 3

Botley

Bampton

Brighthampton

A415

B4017

A4095

Clanfield

A34

B480

A34

A4074

A420

Kingston
Bagpuize

Abingdon

don

A415

A415

River Ock

A338

A34

Sutton
Courtenay

A417

Didcot

A4130

Wantage

A417

B4508

B4507

Harwell

A34

B4001

n

Cholsey

A417

Lambourn

A338

B4494

A34

B4009

Kilometres ――― 8

Miles ――― 5

THE UPPER THAMES

At Thames Head.

The source spring.

The source

A 19.7km walk following 19.6km of the river

Source of the Thames ST 981 995 / GL7 6NZ

Cricklade High Bridge SU 101 940 / SN6 6DA

Introduction

The mighty Thames originates in a quiet corner of the Cotswold Hills. The actual source is unspectacular, being located in a (usually dry) field and marked by a nondescript stone. However, tracing the infant stream's course downstream is a pleasant introduction to the Upper Thames.

Waypoints

Kemble Station ST 985 976 / GL7 6AW

Lay-by on A433/ Fosse Way ST 983 988 / GL7 6NZ

Source of the Thames ST 981 995 / GL7 6NZ

Waterhay Bridge SU 060 933 / SN6 6QY

Cricklade High Bridge SU 101 940 / SN6 6DA

Description

This walk follows the course of the Thames Path National Trail, which commences at the source (and continues 184 miles to the Thames Barrier). There is no need to offer directions as the route is well sign-posted; summarised below are highlights in the river's early development.

To visit the source, either walk 2.5km from the railway station in the village of Kemble (accessible from Lechlade via bus and then train), or 1km from a rough lay-by on the right-hand side of the A433/Fosse Way heading towards Cirencester, encountered just after passing under a railway bridge. Your route

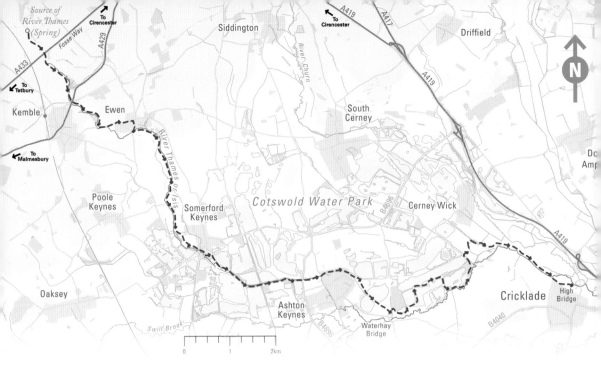

leads you 'upstream' through several fields following the Thames Path in reverse, until you spot your quarry; a stone marker and some wooden signs under an ash tree, located 105.8 m above sea level.

"The Thames rises in a very pretty valley-mead ... its stream issues from between stones in a small well-like hole, shaded by thorny bushes; under some low trees, close to the rising bank of the canal." Henry Taunt,

A New Map of the River Thames 1871

In winter, spring water magically bubbles up as described into a wide pool, forming a 'winterbourne' stream which trickles south across Trewsbury Mead. In summer, the jumble of stones is dry.

"I found only a dried up well ... needless to say I was disappointed." Robert Gibbings,

Sweet Thames Run Softly 1940

Close by is a tediously inscribed plinth: *'The Conservators of the River Thames, 1857–1974. This stone was placed here to mark the source of the River Thames'.* A statue of 'Old Father Thames' was also here, until moved to St John's Lock in 1974.

The canal referred to by Taunt is the long since dried-up Thames & Severn Canal, which passed behind the source atop a raised bank, connecting the Thames at Inglesham to the Severn via the 3,817 yard Sapperton Tunnel under the Cotswold Hills. The canal was built 1783–89, never saw heavy use, and was abandoned in 1927.

Setting out along the Thames Path, you will notice that even in summer, reeds and other water plants survive in the wide hollow marking the river's course. By the time you reach Thames Head on the Fosse Way, there

THE SOURCE

📷 *Through Cotswold Water Park.*

may even be some water visible; in winter a large pool forms. Irritatingly, the Thames Path winds away from the river's course at frequent intervals in the following section; however at a distance of 4.3km from its source, the path rejoins the Thames when it has enough flow for its first mill, which was sited at Mill Farm. Further mill shoots and small weirs follow as you walk along open fields down to Somerford Keynes, where the landscape dramatically changes.

For around ten kilometres the Thames flows among the reservoirs of the Cotswold Water Park www.waterpark.org, which often close in on both sides with only small embankments delineating the river's course. There are around 140 lakes spanning 12,000 acres, the UK's largest marl lake system. The park is a result of limestone gravel quarrying from the 1930s to the present. This industrial landscape is, surprisingly, a beautiful environment, creating a haven for all manner of aquatic wildlife which in turn feeds the Thames ecosystem. For example, the park harbours 13 species of damselflies, all manner of water birds ranging from bitterns to willow warblers, and mammals such as water voles, otters and water shrews. There is a visitor centre (the Gateway Centre) in South Cerney at Spine Road GL7 5TL for those wishing to learn more.

In the centre of the Cotswold Water Park the Thames Path loses the river at the village of Ashton Keynes. A diversion is recommended to Waterhay Bridge, where there is also a car park. If the river actually begins to resemble a river here, it's because Swill Brook has swelled its flow with water flowing from the lakes. A century ago, barges made it upstream to Waterhay Bridge, just 13.4km from the source ... the river must have been much less overgrown!

The Thames Path returns to the river for the last few kilometres into Cricklade. These pass through North Meadow National Nature Reserve, a glorious 112-acre flood meadow which has been used for winter pasture and summer haymaking since Alfred the Great founded Cricklade in 890. This is a rare surviving example of Lammas land, open annually from Lammas (harvest festival time) for Cricklade commoners to communally graze ten cattle or horses; if you happen to be here then (early August), you will witness the annual stampede of animals as they are released into the meadow. North Meadow is the first of the huge flood meadows which characterise of the River Thames all the way down to London, a key part of both the river's ecosystems and charm.

The four-pointed tower of sixteenth-century St Sampson's Church is visible long before you enter Cricklade. This tower was added in 1552 by the Duke of Northumberland, father-in-law of Lady Jane Grey; the following year he installed her as Queen of England and was executed for this nine-day coup.

Cricklade (*'place by river crossing'*) has been around at least since 890, when Alfred the Great fortified it against the Danes. This quiet town at the head of the Thames navigation is an attractive cluster of honey-coloured Cotswold stone buildings, but it received a bad

 In the water.

press in the nineteenth century: "Villainous hole" (William Cobbett, *Rural Rides* 1830) and: "Dull to live in, dull to look at, dull to talk about" (James Thorne, *Rambles by Rivers* 1849). Study the stream rippling below High Bridge, 19.4 kilometres from the source; surely at this point the Thames is well worth a paddle?

In his 1930's guidebooks, William Bliss describes paddling and portaging as far up-stream as Kemble, "We had somehow got to where, I dare swear, no such craft has ever penetrated, before or since", and then drag-ging overland to the source. Modern paddlers attempting similar stunts have experienced both masochism and landowner hostility.

Which source?

Some dispute Trewsbury Mead as the true source. If measured from the source of the River Churn, one of the Cotswold tributaries, the Thames would be 23km longer. This would make it the longest river in the British Isles, at 370km! The Churn source, known as Seven Springs, is higher at 213m and never dries. It is marked by a plaque inscribed in Latin.

HIC TUUS OTAMESINE PATER SEP-TEMGEMINUS FONS

(Oh Father Thames, here is your seven-fold source)

Castle Eaton.

Cricklade to Lechlade

Distance   17km

Start   △ Cricklade SU 103 938 / SN6 6BL

Finish   ◯ Lechlade Riverside Park SU 211 990 / GL7 3AL

Introduction

Exploring the dense green wilderness of the Thames' upper paddleable reaches is an exceptional adventure, assuming you are prepared to accept a bit of a challenge! Consider allocating more than one day to complete this mini-expedition.

Launch points

Cricklade SU 103 938 / SN6 6BL – slipway and small parking area off Abingdon Court Road.
Red Lion in Castle Eaton SU 145 958 / SN6 6JZ – only with prior permission. Eat and drink there out of courtesy!

Hannington Bridge SU 174 961 / SN6 7RX – small lay-by on river left, with a gate beside an Environment Agency measuring station. Use discretion.
Lechlade Riverside Park SU 211 990 / GL7 3AL – car park on river right 200m from the water, off the A361.

Description

This trip is unlike any other part of the Thames; overgrown and fallen trees necessitate innumerable ducks and dodges as well as a number of portages. The channel can become narrow

and overgrown with reeds during summer. Charles Dickens's son noted that it can be "in dry seasons uncomfortably shallow." (Charles Dickens, *Dictionary of the Thames* 1887). Actually it is likely to be floatable year round for paddlecraft; judge at the start whether you have a floatable depth. High water flows are not recommended due to the tree hazards.

Most folk do a double-take when they first walk to the end of the Cricklade slipway, as did William Cobbett.

"I rode through it here, it not being above four or five yards wide, and not deeper than the knees of my horse."

Rural Rides 1830

Even so, in Cobbett's day and for a lifetime beyond, cargo barges docked here. Now, bushes and trees encroach severely in the six kilometres to Castle Eaton; paddlers will be ducking and weaving right from the slipway! The A419 bridge is the last sign of modernity you'll see for several hours once the reeds close in, and the confluence of the River Ray on river right one of few recognisable landmarks. The pace is slow. At time of writing there were perhaps four tree blockages, all of which portageable at river level but more than one involving climbing and lifting. Large groups will clog the stream and struggle to make quick progress.

"I never did such a piece of river in my life. What a pace we went ... a mile an hour at least."

Paul Blake,

The Thames: Oxford to its Source 1888

The reward for this slow and heavy going is access to a secret, green world. Kingfishers abound, the author has spotted water voles and otters here and the air is thick with insects, best described by naturalist Robert Gibbings.

📷 *Picnic below Cricklade.*

"Turquoise dragon flies flit from lily leaf to lily leaf, and the pond skater and those small mer-curial beetles, the whirlygigs, gyrate and skim above the surface of the stream."

Sweet Thames Run Softly 1940

The girders of Castle Eaton Bridge are ugly, but also a relief as henceforth the going is much easier! On river right is the red-brick eighteenth-century Red Lion, the first pub on the Thames and the first potential egress. Shortly past this and behind the willows is St Mary's Church, which has a distinctive bellcote spire in the centre. The church dates from the twelfth century but was renovated by Victorian Gothic revivalist William Butterfield. From Castle Eaton to Lechlade, the Thames follows the Gloucestershire/Wiltshire bound-ary. While still a naturalist's delight, the river is wider and (mostly!) clear. It sweeps quietly behind the village of Kempsford (Old English ford of big marsh), located on river left; from the river you'll spot the remains of Saxon earthworks as well as remnants of a medieval manor. The church tower between these two structures dates from 1390 and was built for John of Gaunt. The past leaves fewer visible traces on river right, but this meadow is known as Battlefield. In 1670, spearheads and other traces were uncovered from a battle which took place around 800AD, here on the border of the Saxon kingdoms of Mercia and Wessex. Enormous military aircraft periodically roar overhead, taking off from or landing at RAF Fairford. This NATO airfield behind Kempsford is leased by the US. The air (and local road) traffic peaks annually in July when the Royal International Air Tattoo is held. With RAF Brize Norton also located 12km to the north-east, the roar of military aircraft is commonplace along the Thames right through to Oxford.

📷 Below Hannington Bridge.

The Thames briefly regresses to a 'treefest' after Hannington Bridge, although no portages are necessary. In the following five kilometres the river becomes deeper and wider and you may see a few moored power boats, for the first time.

When the hamlet of Inglesham is reached on river right, the spire of St Lawrence's Church in Lechlade is already visible across the adjoining meadow. However, consider a jaunt

📷 Round House at Inglesham.

ashore in Inglesham to explore the Church of St John the Baptist with its Saxon artefacts and twelfth-century wall paintings inside; this unusual church owes its survival to William Morris (see Section 2) whose saved it from being 'improved' through his 1877 Society for the Protection of Ancient Buildings, a fore runner of the National Trust.

Shortly past Inglesham on river left at the confluence of the River Coln is the junction of the Thames & Severn Canal, which may eventually be restored. The ramshackle remains of the lock can be viewed from the river. Alongside is the distinctive Round House, which was accommodation for lock keepers and canal workers. There are five more Round Houses along the canal's 46km. Incidentally, this was the furthest point reached by Percy and Mary Shelley on their 1815 rowing expedition from Windsor. They had planned to follow the canal

[📷] *Above Inglesham.*

to the River Severn and beyond, but couldn't afford the canal toll. The Shelleys retreated to Lechlade, where Percy composed the poem *A Summer Evening Churchyard, Lechlade*.

Downstream of the canal is an arched footbridge. The Riverside Park is now on river right, and the Thames veers closest to the car park in about 300m.

If your day began at the knee-deep wadeable Thames of Cricklade, you might well be suffering from exhaustion and culture shock.

Variations

Many will choose to tackle this long section over two days, with a break at Castle Eaton or Hannington Bridge.

Some paddlers have launched or ventured further upstream, encountering heavy going through more tree portages.

📷 *Below Rushey Lock.*

Eaton Footbridge.

Lechlade to Tadpole Bridge

Distance   17.2km

Start   △ Lechlade Riverside Park SU 211 990 / GL7 3AL

Finish   ○ Tadpole Bridge SP 335 004 / SN7 8RF

Introduction

This is the quietest section of the navigable Thames, bending back and forth across lush meadows, far from settlements. Featuring along the route are the Thames' oldest bridges and a surprising (optional) white-water interlude!

Launch points

Lechlade Riverside Park SU 211 990 / GL7 3AL – car park on river right 200m from the water, off the A361.

Lechlade Riverside Inn SU 213 994 / GL7 3AQ – car park river left above Ha'penny Bridge.

A417 Lechlade Road. Small launching area, unsuitable for large groups.

Trout Inn, Lechlade SU 224 990 / GL7 3HA – slipway in camping field on river left below St John's Lock, A417 Lechlade Road. Only with prior permission.

Cheese Wharf SU 224 983 / SN7 8DQ – National Trust picnic spot and parking area on river right, A417 Lechlade Road.

Radcot Bridge SU 285 994 / OX18 2SX – car park between the two bridges. A4095 Radcot Road. Only with prior permission from the Swan Hotel.

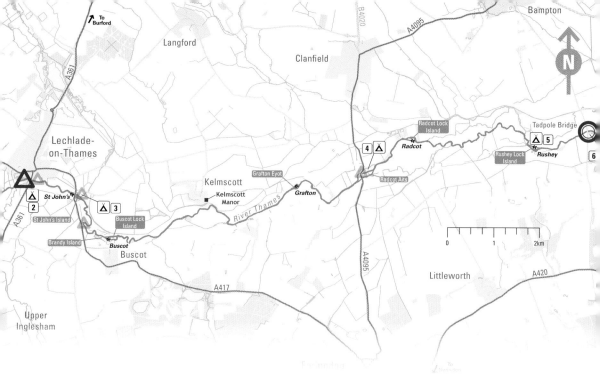

Tadpole Bridge SP 335 004 / SN7 8RF – river left below the bridge onto the Thames Path. Buckland Road. Small lay-by a short distance away.

Description

The town of Lechlade is mostly away from the river, but is fronted by a lively quayside. You may recognise the Riverside Inn from the film which started the London 2012 Olympics opening ceremony!

Ha'penny Bridge forms a shapely bow over the water. The smaller arch was for tow horses. Locals protested after it opened in 1792 as all who crossed (other than Sunday churchgoers) were charged a toll of ... well, the name is a giveaway. The toll keeper's cottage survives on the Gloucestershire side (river left bank), although the bridge has been toll-free since 1875. Four counties meet

around Lechlade; the river left bank changing from Gloucestershire to Oxfordshire, and the river right bank from Wiltshire to Berkshire.

A few meanders across a meadow lead past a pillbox (see boxed text The GHQ Stop Line) on river left (the first of many) to St John's Lock, first opened in 1789. Alongside the lock pound is a statue of Old Father Thames reclining with (for no apparent reason) a spade. This 'Marmite' (you either love it or hate it) figure was sculpted from Portland cement by Rafaelle Monti for the 1851 Great Exhibition. After Crystal Palace went up in flames in 1936, it was relocated to the source at Trewsbury Mead and then in 1974 (after being vandalised) to the lock.

Emerging from the lock, you paddle through a man-made canyon beneath St John's Bridge. The single ivy-strewn arch crossing the

weir on the river left side of St John's Island dates from 1229, placing it among the river's oldest bridges. Overlooking the weir pool is the Trout Inn, built among a few traces of a thirteenth-century priory. The inn's camping field is directly downstream, its slipway hidden a short distance up the River Leach (from which Lechlade takes its name).

The Thames now heads into the sticks; there are no villages or towns on the river until Oxford! In 2000, Bloomer's Hole Footbridge had to be lugged in by Chinook helicopter. It marks the start of a succession of tight bends; keep an eye out for narrowboats which struggle here. A pillbox overlooking a long left bend indicates the imminence of Cheese Wharf, now a picnic spot; 2–3,000 tonnes of its namesake were exported from here annually.

You might glimpse Buscot Church (and its 1703

The GHQ Stop Line

The Upper Thames has the highest concentration of visible World War Two pillboxes along its banks, although large numbers survive hidden in the undergrowth along the whole river. This was General Ironside's GHQ Stop Line, a 500km anti-tank defence which looped from Peterborough around the east and south of London before heading west along the north bank of the Thames. This vast defensive landscape aimed to prevent Blitzkrieg-style encirclement of the capital by Nazi invaders. It was manned by Home Guard volunteers ('Dad's Army'), alongside the Upper Thames Patrol, a division of the Home Guard in small boats (Dad's Navy?), tasked with preventing river crossings.

parsonage) on river right, boasting windows by Edward Burne-Jones. You are paddling through the Buscot Estate, bought in 1859 by Australian gold merchant Robert Campbell and now owned by the National Trust. Campbell dredged the river and installed two waterwheels at nearby Hart's Weir to pump water uphill to his house; schemes such as these led him to eventual bankruptcy. Buscot House is about 700m south of the river. Buscot Lock – at 33m the smallest on the Thames – was first built in 1791, although the weir and its gates date from 1979. Alongside the lock is Brandy Island, where Campbell spent £100,000 setting up an innovative distillery making alcohol from sugar beet. The island has more recently been home to a Thames Water pumping station. Note that the 1:25,000 Ordnance Survey map oddly shows the lock on the wrong channel, but the lock channel is of course obvious on arrival.

A kilometre below the lock, both banks become Oxfordshire and then Eaton Footbridge is reached. The river splits into channels which were clearly once a lock, known as Hart's Weir. This was removed in 1938.

A sign beside a long right bend indicates that you are passing Kelmscott Manor on river left, home of eminent Victorian William Morris. A short footpath leads to the manor and Morris' grave is 800m from the river, with a pub conveniently located midway.

The two kilometres to Grafton Lock pass the eleventh-century Church of St Michael and All Angels at Eaton Hastings. This is out of sight in the trees on right, but is notable for windows

[📷] Brandy Lock.

📷 *Grafton Lock.*

by Morris, Burne-Jones and Ford Madox Ford. With its 1896 lock keeper's cottage, manicured lawns and immaculate flower beds, Grafton Lock is – like many locks to follow – a startling interlude of orderly Englishness after kilometres of overgrown and unmanaged banks. The river splits at the Radcot Aits. The river left channel is the navigation channel, passing under New Radcot Bridge to the Swan Hotel. This single arch underwent substantial recent reconstruction after a lorry nearly destroyed it. It has also taken some hits from powerboats which struggle with the tight bend above. This channel and bridge are actually an artificial addition from 1787, cut through the centre of an island. There is another (narrow and overgrown) channel further left, while the river right channel was originally the main course of the river, passing under attractive Radcot

Bridge, which is guarded by an incongruous WWII bunker. This is the strongest contender for the oldest surviving Thames bridge, with two of its three arches dating from around 1200. The central arch is the youngster, rebuilt after the Battle of Radcot Bridge in 1387, when Robert De Vere's army, representing King Richard II, was encircled and defeated by rebel barons.

Flash locks – the bad old days

Before the present lock was built, Grafton Eyot was the site of one of the upper river's flash locks. These were notorious both for the challenges presented by riding the surge of whitewater downstream when the central slats were removed, and by hauling upstream against the unleashed torrent.

Radcot Lock is 1.5km downstream and hides a surprise. It is possible to bypass the 1892 lock by following the 'Canoe Pass' channel on river left above. Amazingly, a 300m-long miniature whitewater course has been landscaped around the lock. This winds tortuously along reed banks over small riffles, before unceremoniously flushing paddlers out below the weir. Splendid fun, and despite the excitement, nothing much can go wrong here (usual disclaimers apply).

The first landmark below Radcot Weir is Old Man's Bridge, another high footbridge. The five kilometres to Tadpole Bridge flow to and fro around a seemingly endless series of bends between reed shores, with distant pylons being the only clue to the century until Rushey Lock. The weir which you will glimpse before taking the river left lock channel is the oldest 'paddle and rymer' weir in the country, one of only three left on the Thames. As you'll see, the weir flow is controlled by lifting and lowering a series of vertical slats; paddles and rymers. The lock is a lovely quiet spot for a picnic, the keeper's house dating from 1894 with a distinctive pyramidal roof.

It's now just a kilometre to the high, single arch of Tadpole Bridge.

Variations

A relaxing hour or two could be passed exploring the back channels around the Radcot Aits, which are inhabited mainly by wildfowl and terns.

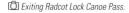 *Exiting Radcot Lock Canoe Pass.*

📷 *Kelmscott Manor.*

Kelmscott Manor

William Morris lived here from 1869 until his death in 1896. Visiting is something of a pilgrimage for devotees of his 'Arts and Crafts' movement. The manor is 'Utopia' in his socialist novel *News from Nowhere*, and many of his iconic wallpaper designs (e.g. 'Willow Bough') were inspired by the river. Morris shared Kelmscott with his wife Jane and best friend Dante Gabriel Rossetti. Jane was muse and lover to the laudanum-addicted Pre-Raphaelite painter,

making for an awkward *ménage à trois*! The house is still crammed with Morris' furniture and textiles, and a visit offers insights into his craft and philosophies.

"What better place than this then could we find
By this sweet stream that knows not of the sea,
That guesses not the city's misery,
This little stream whose hamlets scarce have names,
This far-off, lonely mother of the Thames?"

Earthly Paradise, William Morris

Newbridge.

Tadpole Bridge to Bablock Hythe

Distance	15.5km
Start	△ Tadpole Bridge SP 335 004 / SN7 8RF
Finish	○ Bablock Hythe SP 435 042 / OX29 5AT

Introduction

If you enjoyed the solitude and quiet on the section above, you'll be entranced by this, the remotest part of the entire river.

Launch points

Tadpole Bridge SP 335 004 / SN7 8RF – river left below the bridge onto the Thames Path. Buckland Road. There is a small lay-by a short distance away.

Newbridge SP 404 014 / OX29 7QD – awkward, a traffic hotspot. A415 Abingdon Road. Possible on river left by parking some distance down the side road and carrying 100m up the Windrush Path (opposite the Rose Revived Inn) and launching into the River Windrush. Or, seek permission from the Maybush Inn to use their car park on river right.

Bablock Hythe SP 435 042 / OX29 5AT – quiet parking area on river right beside the river. End of Bablock Hythe Road.

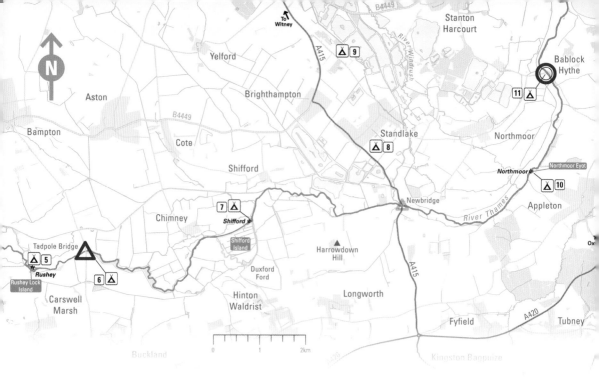

Description

You launch on river left below Tadpole Bridge, opposite the Trout Inn. The bridge dates from 1789. The river is soon swallowed up by the reeds and trees, with no landmarks for three kilometres until Tenfoot Bridge (a footbridge). Less than two kilometres further, and you reach Shifford Lock Cut; the channel splits with river right falling over a weir, while the navigation channel ahead curves uniformly to the left for around 800m. This artificial channel was dug in 1896–7, to bypass a large meandering loop. Although man-made, today it is a gorgeous tunnel of greenery, passing beneath a footbridge before it reaches Shifford Lock, below which the two channels reunite. On river right is uninhabited Shifford Island, created by the Lock Cut. Shifford Lock was the last to be built on the river, in 1898. This is the most

remote spot on the Thames, only accessible on foot; as recently as the 1940s, the lock keeper was self-sufficient, cultivating crops and keeping animals.

Below Shifford Lock, the original river channel rejoins from river right, alongside a weir. Shifford Lock takes its name from the hamlet of Shifford, located away from the river about

📷 *Tadpole Bridge.*

📷 *Shifford Lock Cut.*

a kilometre downstream on river left. The name means 'sheep ford', and hereabouts in 890, Alfred the Great reputedly presided over one of the first English parliaments.

It is another three kilometres to Newbridge. Harrowdown Hill is a lonely landmark on river right. This secluded spot tragically entered the national news in 2003, during the Iraq War 'dodgy dossier' controversy; UN Weapons Inspector Dr David Kelly was found dead here. Newbridge – with its busy traffic and two pubs – feels like a teeming metropolis after

Chimney Meadows Nature Reserve

Why is this stretch so idyllically peaceful? Stretching for around four kilometres from 500m before Tenfoot Bridge to 500m after Shifford Lock, the river left bank is Chimney Meadows Nature Reserve, at 261 hectares the largest run by Berks, Bucks & Oxon Wildlife Trust www.bbowt.org.uk. This vast reserve also includes Shifford Island on the opposite bank. The site of a former farm,

Chimney Meadows is home to a wide range of species: roe deer hide in the trees, bats roost in pillboxes, wildflowers bloom in the ancient meadows, while little egret, little grebe and kingfisher thrive in the wetlands. Time out to walk and explore a little is recommended; a camp at Shifford Lock is one splendid way to do this.

📷 *Northmoor Lock.*

the previous ten kilometres! The River Windrush joins on river left upstream of the bridge, which boasts six arches and has been here since c.1250. Its name only makes sense in relation to its older neighbour, Radcot Bridge! The Maybush Inn is above the bridge on river right, and the larger Rose Revived Inn is downstream on river left, shielded by an impressive wall of weeping willow. The

Rose Revived's name recalls a visit by Oliver Cromwell, who supposedly dipped the rose he was wearing into his pint. Whether this story is true or not, in 1644 the bridge (guarding the approach to Royalist Oxford) was certainly the site of a Civil War skirmish.

Two kilometres after the bridge, you arrive at Hart's Footbridge. After making progress eastwards thus far, the Thames now trends northwards in a loop around the Cumnor Hills. A large house on river right is a somewhat jarring sight (although huge properties will eventually become commonplace), followed by a succession of smaller properties. These are outliers of the village of Appleton, a kilometre uphill.

The river splits around Northmoor Eyot with its line of planted poplars; this is Northmoor

📷 *Newbridge.*

📷 *Camping at Northmoor Lock.*

Lock, with a campsite on river right. The lock dates from 1896 and has the third and final of the surviving manually-operated 'paddle and rymer' weirs alongside (the others are at Rushey and Radcot). The road here is only for campsite internees, so (unless camping) you'll need to float another pleasant couple of kilometres to end the trip at Bablock Hythe Road, on river right opposite a hotel.

Variations

An exploration of the **Duxford Loop** around Shifford Island will take you into some of the Thames' quietest waters! A kilometre or so upstream from Shifford Lock is Duxford Ford, the last on the river heading downstream. A portage may be required if you wish to bushwhack even further upstream, but you will certainly be guaranteed the river to yourself.

Youth group at Bablock Hythe.

Bablock Hythe to Oxford

Distance 19.1km

Start △ Bablock Hythe SP 435 042 / OX29 5AT

Finish ◯ Riverside Centre SP 524 044 / OX4 4AZ

Introduction

The approach to Oxford is steeped in natural beauty. The city itself does not present its best side to the river, but the urban interlude is brief and there are more nature reserves per kilometre through Oxford than on any other part of the Thames!

Launch points

Bablock Hythe SP 435 042 / OX29 5AT – quiet parking area beside the river. End of Bablock Hythe Road.

Wolvercote SP 487 094 / OX2 8PG – car park with height barrier. Godstow Road.

Osney Bridge SP 503 062 / OX2 0AU – river right from East Street. Central Oxford, busy.

Riverside Centre SP 524 044 / OX4 4AZ – Oxford Council slipway off Meadow Lane on river left upstream of the B4495 bridge. Parking beside both Sea Cadets and Falcon Canoe Club buildings, the latter with height barriers.

Description

Bablock Hythe is one of a number of ancient ferry spots surviving along the Thames, invaluable to paddlers. There was probably a ferry here in Roman times; a Roman stone

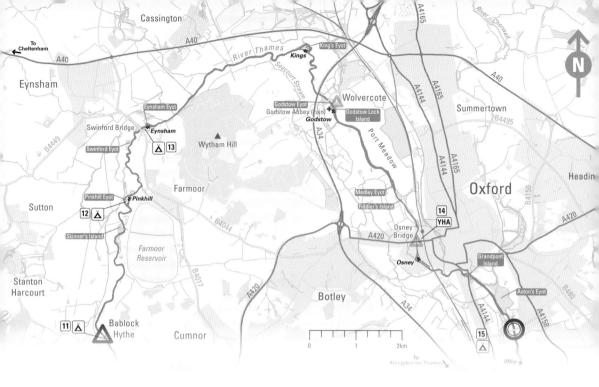

altar found in the river is now in Oxford's Ashmolean Museum. The river left shore of the ferry is the bland Ferryman Inn, the start of a bland caravan park along the next kilometre. The river then avoids conurbation for over a dozen kilometres.

The Thames winds north alongside the high bank of river right Farmoor Reservoir, created in 1976. There are two nature reserves in front of Farmoor; Shrike Meadow and Pinkhill Meadow are a series of lagoons and ponds which merge with the Thames in high flows. In between the two is the marshy woodland of Skinner's Island.

Pinkhill Lock was built in 1898 around Pinkhill Eyot, on which it is possible to camp. From here to Swinford Bridge, the only thing of note is Swinford Eyot, created by one of many tight meanders. Exploring its overgrown back

channel, you might glimpse a house and private helipad(!) on the island.

Swinford Bridge was built in 1777, after John Wesley nearly drowned (1764) and King George III fell into the river (1769) while crossing. (This is one of three toll bridges on the Thames, the others being at Whitchurch and Dartford.) Traffic is busy and landing/launching is not very practical. Just downstream is Eynsham Lock, dating from 1928.

The Thames describes a great arc around 165m Wytham Hill, dominating the river right bank. This is densely covered by Wytham Great Wood, a 388-hectare ancient forest which since 1942 has been left near-wild by Oxford University as an ecological research station (www.wytham.ox.ac.uk). This amazing sylvan enclave has huge biodiversity with, for example, over 800 species of moths and

📷 *Pinkhill Lock.*

butterflies. There is an entrance 400m from Eynsham Lock; visitors need to apply in advance for a free walking permit.

The Thames becomes notably wider approaching Oxford. Many streams criss-cross the meadows around; Wharf Stream joins on river left, followed by the Cassington Cut, a disused canal to the River Evenlode. The Evenlode next joins, last of the Cotswold tributaries. At a tight bend known as Hagley Pool, Seacourt Stream (aka. Wytham Stream) leaves via a weir to flow south, bypassing Oxford while interlinking with a bewildering array of flood relief streams before rejoining the Thames below Oxford; Botley Stream, Bulstrake Stream, Hogacre Ditch, Hinksey Stream, Weirs Mill Stream and there are more! Yarnton Mead is delightful, despite the audible A40; butterflies and marsh orchids abound, while larks soar above. As the Thames reaches its northernmost point at wooded King's Eyot, a channel branches off on river left around Pixey Mead, rejoining at Wolvercote; this channel is connected to the Oxford Canal via the Duke's Cut, making various 'loop' paddles possible. At King's Lock (1928) there is a wood and hay bale hut with interesting displays on the river's natural and human history.

The A34 roars above across Thames Bridge (a 1961 concrete slab), but the river refuses to be urbanised just yet. The following three kilometres are celebrated by some as the Thames' finest! Incidentally, some locals insist on referring to the Thames from here to Iffley Lock as the Isis.

📷 *Godstow Abbey.*

"Godstow Bridge is highly picturesque; the river divide here, and at the brink of the older and more shallow channel is a pleasant Inn 'The Trout', well known to anglers, but better to the Oxford scholar."   Mr and Mrs S.C. Hall,
The Book of the River Thames 1859

The Thames splits once more around Godstow Eyot. The river left channel flows under the two arches of the older (c.1692) Godstow Bridge and directly over a weir. On river left below, the Trout Inn is famous for the peacocks roaming the beer garden and as a favourite hangout of Oxford undergraduates, and also Inspector Morse. The river right lock cut was dug and bridged in 1792. The cut leads past the ruins of Godstow Abbey to Godstow Lock, the first electric lock on the Thames; henceforth, lock operation is simpler,

but you will miss the nostalgic pleasure of manual operation!

Below Godstow Lock, it is possible to finish at Wolvercote, where JRR Tolkien is buried. The river now skirts the vast expanse of Wolvercote Common and Port Meadow, c.170 hectares of uncultivated pasture stretching along over two kilometres of the river left bank.

Grazing rights on this remarkable common land belong to the folk of Wolvercote and Oxford, the latter privilege granted by Alfred the Great! The meadows have seen various uses (e.g. this was an airstrip during World War One), but remarkably have not been ploughed for at least 4,000 years. You'll be surprised how low-lying the land is; below kayak head height. The only prominence is the Round Hill Bronze Age burial mound. The centre of Port

Godstow Abbey

Godstow Abbey was built c.1133 and destroyed by Cromwell's troops in 1645. Henry II met his great love Rosamund Clifford at the nunnery. After she died in 1176 (possibly poisoned by Queen Eleanor), Henry had her buried before the altar. A disapproving later abbot reburied her elsewhere so that "other women, warned by her example, may refrain from unlawful love". 'Fair Rosamund' supposedly haunts the Trout Inn as a white lady, but actually ghosts aren't real.

In 1862, Charles Dodgson rowed to the Abbey with three children, for a picnic. The story he told them was eventually published under the pseudonym Lewis Carroll as *Alice in Wonderland*. This opens with a poem:

All in the golden afternoon
Full leisurely we glide;
For both our oars, with little skill,
By little arms are plied,
While little hands make vain pretence
Our wanderings to guide.

Meadow floods for months at a time allowing waders to over-winter, with redshank and oystercatchers remaining in the summer. Other perennial residents include greylag geese, herons and little egrets. In 2012, Port Meadow's celebrated backdrop of Oxford's 'dreaming spires' was senselessly obscured by eight garish university student blocks.

The river right bank is also worthy of attention; coots and great-crested grebes nest below

 Port Meadow.

📷 *Oxford above Osney Lock.*

the bushes. Where the river bends left, a path leads into the village of Binsey and the seventeenth-century Perch Inn.

You'll be confused by the following stretch, but when in doubt just keep heading straight ahead and following the navigation signs! Medley Footbridge links narrow Medley Eyot to the river right shore, before the river splits around much larger Fiddler's Island. River left leads under the 1865 arch of Rainbow Bridge via Castle Mill Stream towards Oxford Canal. Stay right following a surprisingly green and tree-lined corridor into Oxford. A crossroads is encountered at the 'Four Streams'; the Sheepwash Channel (formerly the Thames' main channel) leads river left to the canal and Louse Lock (aka Isis Lock), Bulstake Stream leads away river right.

A row of graffitied terraced houses on river left indicates that you are finally in town! The Thames is narrow and canal-like, hemmed in by mills and housing. A 1950's travelogue described this as "a mile of squalor", but nowadays the river is clean and the area somewhat gentrified. Those recalling the old Waterman's Arms on river right will find that it has been refurbished into The Punter.

Osney Bridge is a single, low (2.28m) iron span from 1889, barring large boats from the upper river. Osney Lock was originally built in 1790 by inmates from Oxford Castle Prison; various streams rejoin the river over the following few hundred metres to Osney Railway Bridge. The banks briefly green up again, with river right Grandpont Nature Reserve being a reclaimed gas works site. Count off

📷 *Radcliffe Camera, Oxford.*

two footbridges before Grandpont Island, spanned by the rather fine Folly Bridge, built c.1825. On the island, look for the red-brick building with statues in niches; in the nineteenth century, these indicated that it was a brothel. There are three tunnels under the bridge to investigate.

Christ Church Meadow opens up on river left, giving a view of Oxford University's 'dreaming spires'. Christ Church and Merton College are prominent, as well as the dome of the Radcliffe Camera. More can be seen by exploring up the River Cherwell which joins on river left via two streams. Between them is an imposing line of college boathouses, and you will almost always share this stretch of river with rowers. Rowing activity peaks during Eights Week in late May.

The final stretch to the B4495 Donnington Road Bridge passes Aston's Eyot on river left. Once a rubbish tip, this nature reserve is now a haven for bats, shrews, roe and muntjac deer. The clubhouse of Falcon CC is then reached, with the Riverside Centre next door.

Variations

Paddlers have ventured into **Seacourt Stream** and the surrounding maze of channels, encountering tree blockages, weirs, metal grating and other arduous challenges; venture forth with care.

A more sedate adventure can be enjoyed by paddling the loop formed by the **Oxford Canal** and the Thames from King's Lock to the 'Four Streams', linked up by Louse Lock and the Duke's Cut.

Below Clifton Hampden.

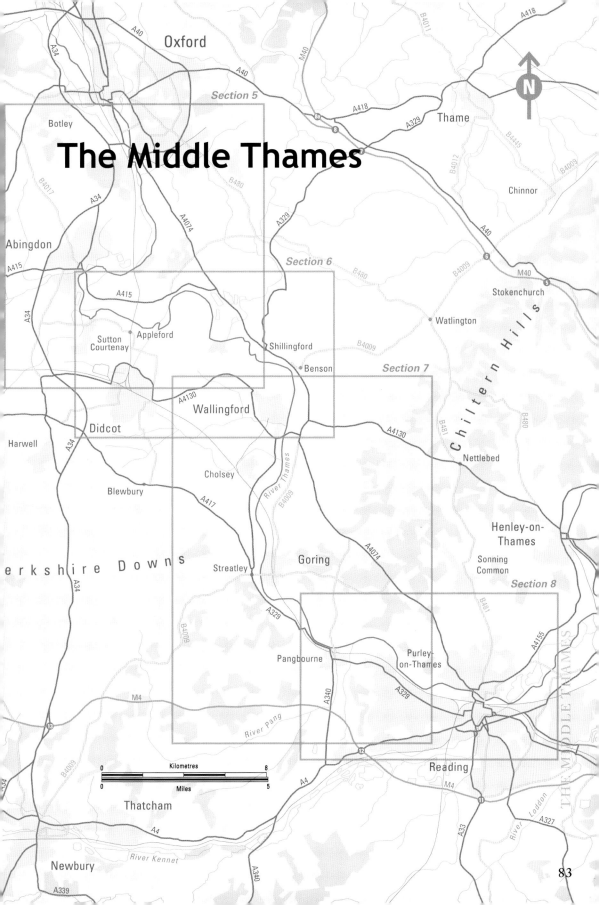

The Middle Thames

Oxford

Section 5

Botley

Abingdon

Sutton
Courtenay

Appleford

Section 6

Shillingford

Benson

Didcot

Harwell

Wallingford

Cholsey

Blewbury

River Thames

Section 7

Thame

Chinnor

Stokenchurch

Watlington

Chiltern Hills

Nettlebed

Henley-on-
Thames

Sonning
Common

Section 8

erkshire Downs

Streatley

Goring

Pangbourne

Purley-
on-Thames

River Pang

Reading

Thatcham

Kilometres
0   8
0   5
Miles

River Kennet

Newbury

River Loddon

THE MIDDLE THAMES

N

© Sutton Bridge.

Oxford to Culham

Distance 15.2km

Start △ Riverside Centre SP 524 044 / OX4 4AZ

Finish ○ Sutton Bridge SU 508 949 / OX14 3BN

Introduction

"No words could convey any adequate idea of the loveliness that gathers about the trees, the meadows, the cultivated fields and slopes, the old homesteads, the thatched roofs."

James S. Whitman,
Down the Thames in a Birch-Bark Canoe 1881

Whitman, an American tourist, rather liked this reach of the Thames. As little has changed since 1881, it's likely that you will too.

Launch points

Riverside Centre SP 524 044 / OX4 4AZ – Oxford Council slipway off Meadow Lane on river left upstream of the B4495 bridge. Parking beside both Sea Cadets and Falcon Canoe Club buildings, the latter with height barriers.

Abingdon Bridge SU 499 968 / OX14 5EJ – beside car park on river left below the bridge. A415 Bridge Street.

Sutton Bridge SU 508 949 / OX14 3BN – car park with height barrier on river left. Tollgate Road.

Description

With its constant B4495 traffic and graffiti-streaked concrete, Donnington Bridge is a contender for the Thames' least appealing

85

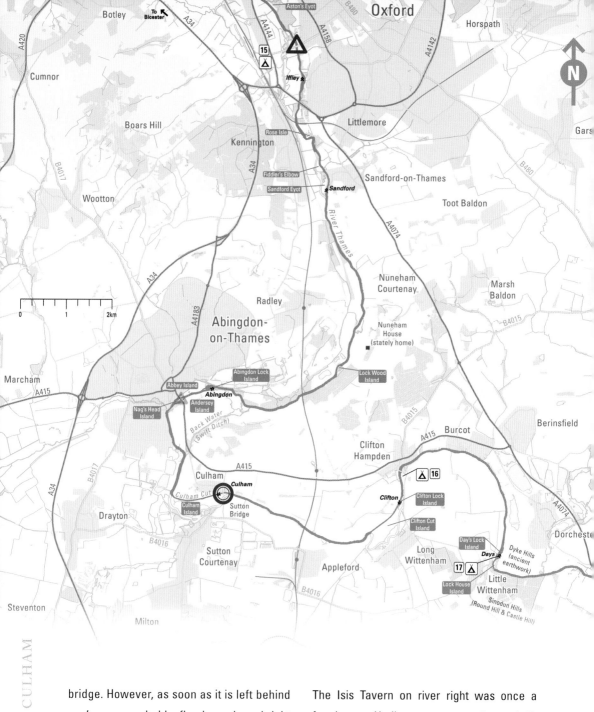

bridge. However, as soon as it is left behind you're surrounded by flood meadows bright with fritillaries and cuckoo flowers; on river left are the tangled brambles of Meadow Lane Nature Park and on river right are Iffley Meadows.

The Isis Tavern on river right was once a farmhouse. Until an access road was built in 1979, it was remote enough for the beer to have to be shipped in! Just below is Iffley Lock, built in 1924, but with traces of a much older pound lock.

📷 Iffley Lock.

Iffley Lock really is quite beautiful! The geese wander freely, the flowers appear to bloom brighter than usual and the footbridge over the boat rollers is (for some reason) a copy of Newton's Bridge at Queen's College, Cambridge. The bronze bull head is the 'starting ring', presented to Oxford University Boat Club in 1924 and traditionally the start point of regatta races. Should you go wandering, Iffley village is close by on river left, with a small shop and the attractive Norman (1170) church of St Mary the Virgin.

The A423 Isis Bridge (a final dose of graffiti art) and disused Kennington Railway Bridge are the last reminders of the city. The meadows below are in the care of the Oxford Preservation Society; Kennington Meadows on river right, and on river left Simon's Land and Heyford Meadow. These surround Rose Isle, a privately-owned island whose lone house was once an inn popular with river traffic.

The main channel now leads left of two long islands; Fiddler's Elbow and then Sandford Eyot, leading to Sandford Lock. The islands can be explored on foot, and hidden behind is lovely Sandford Pool. If you want to reach the pool by boat, best approach from downstream having passed through the lock ... above the pool is the 'Sandford Lasher', the Thames' most notorious weir. Jerome K. Jerome for once wasn't joking when he described it as "a very good place to drown yourself in." (*Three Men in a Boat* 1889). Atop the weir is an obelisk commemorating

📷 *Nuneham House.*

students from Christ Church College who have drowned here. These five men include Michael Llywelyn Davies, J.M. Barrie's adopted son and the inspiration for *Peter Pan*. He died alongside his lover in 1921, in a suspected suicide pact.

"One of the most picturesque of the many combinations of lock, weir and mill."

Mr and Mrs S.C. Hall,
The Book of the River Thames 1859

Sandford Lock is found towards the end of Sandford Eyot, just before the weir stream rejoins. This is the non-tidal river's deepest lock, a clue to the Lasher's severity. Its 2.7m drop feels like a startling height from within a canoe! On river left is The King's Arms pub. The mill buildings around are converted to housing, but date from the 1620s, with traces originally built in the

thirteenth century for the Knights Templar.

A long quiet stretch follows. Radley College Boat House is the first riverside building for three kilometres, at which point you also glimpse a fine stately home atop the hill on river left. This is Nuneham House and the river follows Nuneham Park for the next kilometre, passing the estate's boathouse with its distinctive pointed roof. Nuneham House was built in 1756 for the Harcourt family, with grounds landscaped by Lancelot 'Capability' Brown. Queen Victoria and Prince Albert had their honeymoon here, declaring it to be "a most lovely place". Henry Taunt was entranced by Nuneham: "a series of beautiful pictures such as only nature can produce." (*A New Map of the River Thames* 1871). The house now belongs to Oxford University.

Shortly after your final view back to Nuneham House, the river left hillside closes to the water's edge as you come to Lock Wood Island. Charles Dodgson (aka Lewis Carroll) picnicked on this large island with Alice Liddell. Just downstream is a tiny one-tree island, marked out during the author's last paddle by a huge pirate flag!

A further three kilometres of undeveloped river lead to Abingdon Lock, the only modern intrusion being at Nuneham Railway Bridge (aka Black Bridge). You will notice two small channels leading off on river left, over weirs; these are the start of Back Water, informally known as 'Swift Ditch'. This two kilometre ... well, ditch, bypasses Abingdon (forming 110 hectare Andersey Island) to rejoin at Culham Bridge. It is amazing to learn that weeny Swift Ditch was the original course of the Thames! Around 955, monks began diverting flow to Abingdon. Swift Ditch remained the navigation channel, with the Thames' first pound lock built there c.1630; traces remain today. The Ditch was finally bypassed in 1790, when the channel to Abingdon was widened and the new lock built there.

The current Abingdon Lock dates from 1905. On river right above the weir, Abbey Stream leads off around Abbey Island, rejoining above Abingdon Bridge; careful exploring is possible, but the stream terminates under old mill buildings. The seventh-century abbey responsible for diverting the Thames was dissolved by Henry VIII in 1538, with only the gatehouse surviving today, on the island.

Below Abingdon Lock.

📷 *Abingdon Church.*

Abingdon Bridge (aka Burford Bridge) hails back to 1790, but was rebuilt in 1927. It spans Nag's Head Island, named for the pub at its north-east end. The town of Abingdon occupies the river right bank for the next kilometre, with the 46m spire of St Helen's Church the centrepiece of a not unattractive backdrop. Just past the church, the River Ock joins at St Helen's Wharf, beneath a little cast iron bridge of 1824, inscribed by the Wilts & Berks Canal Company. The canal is now gone, but attempts have begun to restore it; downstream of Abingdon you will spot a short stump leading off to the right. There is a little weir a short way up the Ock, should you fancy a diversion. After the entrance to Abingdon Marina is passed on river right and Swift Ditch rejoins on river left, you are back in the Oxfordshire wilds. The river splits around Culham Island, with the navigation channel being along the river left Culham Cut. Dug out in 1809, this bypasses the village of Sutton Courtenay in a one kilometre shortcut to Culham Lock. This takes you efficiently to the end of this section, but it would be a shame to miss the Sutton Pools; see opposite.

📷 *Abingdon Bridge.*

Swift Ditch is a popular paddle, often done as a loop from Abingdon. However, it is overgrown and the weirs require paddling or (awkwardly) portaging, so it is only appropriate for those familiar with moving water.

The back channel behind Culham Island leads to the **Sutton Pools**, three willow-draped weir pools. 1930's kayaker Geoffrey Boumphrey described these as an "enchanting place ... all sorts of small back-waters, islands and isthmuses to explore." (*Down River* 1936). It is easy to visit from downstream, turning right just after Culham Lock and paddling under shapely Sutton Bridge. You can also approach from upstream, taking the river right channel above Culham Island. Proceed with care above several weirs before portaging across the islands. River right are the gardens of some rather nice Sutton Courtenay houses; the distinctive gabled house was home to Herbert Asquith (Prime Minister from 1908–16, buried in the village). You might glimpse the

Sutton Pools.

dinosaurs adorning the garden of (separated) Hollywood couple Tim Burton and Helena Bonham-Carter. Eric Arthur Blair (better known by his pen name, George Orwell) was buried in the churchyard here, despite no local connections.

Day's Lock.

Culham to Wallingford

Distance   17.6km

Start   △ Sutton Bridge SU 508 949 / OX14 3BN

Finish   ○ Wallingford SU 610 894 / OX10 0BL

Introduction

An exceptionally scenic bimble through Oxfordshire's backcountry. This is one of the author's favourites.

Launch points

Sutton Bridge SU 508 949 / OX14 3BN – car park with height barrier on river left. Tollgate Road.

Clifton Hampden SU 547 955 / OX14 3EE – park on lay-by on High Street beside church (not Sunday mornings), river left below bridge.

Shillingford Bridge SU 597 921 / OX10 7EU - possible from Thames Path on river left below the bridge, but no parking close by.

Benson SU 614 915 / OX10 6SH – Rivermead Recreational Area, river left just downstream of The Waterfront Café. Parking area across the A4074.

Wallingford Bridge SU 610 894 / OX10 0BL – beach on river left downstream of bridge. Car park with barrier at Riverside Park, or park on road outside. Track leading off The Street.

Description

Launching below Culham Lock, you pass under the bridge and rejoin the Sutton Pools backwater. The following five kilometres are

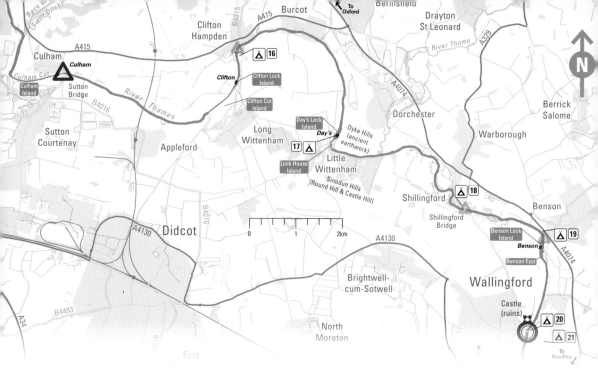

quiet and rural, with only Appleford Railway Bridge to disturb the peace. Enjoy!

The river enters another artificial course after a weir falls away on river right; this is Clifton Cut, dug in 1822 and creating Clifton Cut Island. The 900m Cut leads to Clifton Lock, built on the site of a ferry.

Clifton Hampden Bridge is a contender for 'most attractive Thames Bridge'. Six red-brick arches span the river at a point where it widens over shallows, due to the undredgeable sandstone bed; barges sometimes had to unload here to float across. George Gilbert Scott's 1864 design reflected the Victorian Gothic Revival. The bridge replaced a ferry and still charged a toll until 1946; you can see the toll-keeper's house alongside. The Barley Mow Pub on the river right bank was patronised by Jerome K. Jerome's hapless characters in *Three Men in a Boat* and Clifton

Hampden described as "a wonderfully pretty village, old-fashioned, peaceful, and dainty with flowers, the river scenery is rich and beautiful". The spire overlooking the bridge on river left signifies 1844 St Michael's Church, perched atop a sandstone outcrop. Samuel Ireland saw an earlier incarnation of the church (which has existed since the twelfth century), but his words are still appropriate.

"... the combination of objects is truly pictur-esque. A small church situated on a richly varie-gated bank, rising almost perpendicularly on the border of the river cannot but attract the eye."

Picturesque Views on the River Thames 1791
It's worth landing to visit the churchyard. Search for the grave of William Dyke, whose claim to fame is having (accidentally) fired the opening shot at the Battle of Waterloo. He was court-martialled, but later pardoned by Wellington.

📷 *Approaching Day's Lock.*

A kilometre past Clifton Hampden, the river left shore passes behind Burcot. The lawns of various expensive properties lead to the water. The house fronted by a boathouse was where poet John Masefield ("I must go down to the sea again ... ") lived until his death in 1967, although Masefield's home burned down and has been rebuilt. The river right shore has less to see, but is much more interesting. Clifton Meadows stretch as an open expanse towards two rounded hills. Their outline is unmistakeable to Oxfordshire locals; these are the Sinodun Hills (Celtic – *old fort*), also variously known as the Wittenham Clumps, Berkshire Bubs or Mother Dunch's Buttocks (don't ask). The Thames slowly sketches out a four-kilometre bend until they eventually fill and dominate the view ahead. The western top is Round Hill and the eastern top is Castle Hill, recognisable by its Iron Age earthworks. They enjoy spectacular views of the surrounding countryside and if you have the time, a walk up from Day's Lock to this beauty spot is highly recommended.

Day's Lock has the distinction of having hosted the World Pooh Sticks Championships on numerous occasions since 1983. Yes, apparently that is a 'thing'. The lock was constructed in 1789 and rebuilt in 1871, its name recalling the old toll system. This quiet spot is frequented only by walkers and passing boats (and the lock keeper residing in his 1928 house on the island) but this was a well populated place in prehistory; the hill-fort above the river's bend on river right overlooked the 'Dyke Hills' on river left, two huge earthen banks enclosing a settlement. An Iron Age sword found in the river at the lock hints at this mysterious past.

📷 *Shillingford.*

Past the lock, Little Wittenham Wood falls steeply down to the river. You'll usually spot a heron or kingfisher or two along this reserve, which is run by the Earth Trust. The River Thame emerges from reeds on river left. Despite millennia of the whole river being called Thames, some Tudor writers asserted that only here was the true start of the Thames (where the so-called Isis and Thame joined) and Victorians later picked up on that myth. They were all wrong. There now, I've said it.

After such a long stretch of rural beauty, a vast ostentatious mansion on river left causes culture shock. There will be plenty more of these on the Lower Thames, but for now, they still surprise. Shortly below is Shillingford Bridge, three rather elegant balustraded stone arches from 1827. At the foot of the river right hillside are the immaculate lawns of Shillingford Bridge Hotel.

A near-straight two kilometres leads to Benson. You pass the grounds of Rush Court on river right, fronted on the river by intriguing stone walls and steps. Shortly after, the river left waterfront comes to life, firstly with a campsite, then with a busy marina and café. The small park after the café offers a possible egress. 150m from the river is St Helen's Church, where the tower clock quirkily has two 11s; one of the nines was accidentally painted upside-down as XI. RAF Benson is nearby, a huge helicopter base.

Benson Lock dates from 1788, and was replaced in 1870. The adjacent weir curves around a large pool to connect with Benson Eyot; this pleasant spot was sketched by J.M.W. Turner.

"The gentle fall of its waters, forming a continual cascade, connects a pleasing section of objects, highly worthy of the exertions of an artist."

Samuel Ireland,

Picturesque Views on the River Thames 1791

A near-straight 1.5 kilometres leads to Wallingford Bridge. The farmland around is where, in 1701, Jethro Tull invented and tested his 'seed drill', opening the way to modern agriculture. On river left, Howbery Park is glimpsed; this business park includes (HR) Hydraulic Research Wallingford, now privatised but effectively the UK's main riverine science facility.

A few traces of Wallingford Castle adorn the earthworks on river right, among meadows unaltered for five centuries.

There is a campsite opposite Wallingford Castle on river left. Just below is Wallingford Bridge, a rather epic edifice at 274m long and seventeen arches! Parts of the bridge hail from the thirteenth century, but the three balustraded middle arches were constructed in 1809. Behind on river right is the fine 'pierced' spire of St Peter's Church, experimental Baroque architecture from 1777.

Wallingford.

Variations

The winding channel behind **Clifton Cut Island** can be paddled up from below. After a kilometre, the Plough Inn at Long Wittenham is reached, via a long garden stretching to the river. Few get further!

The **River Thame** usually has a clear enough channel to paddle up a kilometre or so to the historic town of Dorchester. This was the Roman town of Dorocina and from AD 634, the first city of Wessex. Pagan King Cynegils was baptised in the Thames by Birinius, who founded Dorchester Abbey. This somehow survived Henry VIII and is worth a visit today, along with its splendid tea rooms.

Wallingford Castle

Constructed in 1067 alongside an ancient ford, the castle played a pivotal role in the twenty-year 'Anarchy'. In 1142, Queen Matilda arrived after escaping from Oxford barefoot across the frozen Thames and in 1153, the Treaty of Wallingford was signed here, ending this bloody *Game of Thrones*-style struggle. The castle was finally destroyed after a *different* Civil War; this was the last part of Oxfordshire to hold out against Cromwell, falling in 1646.

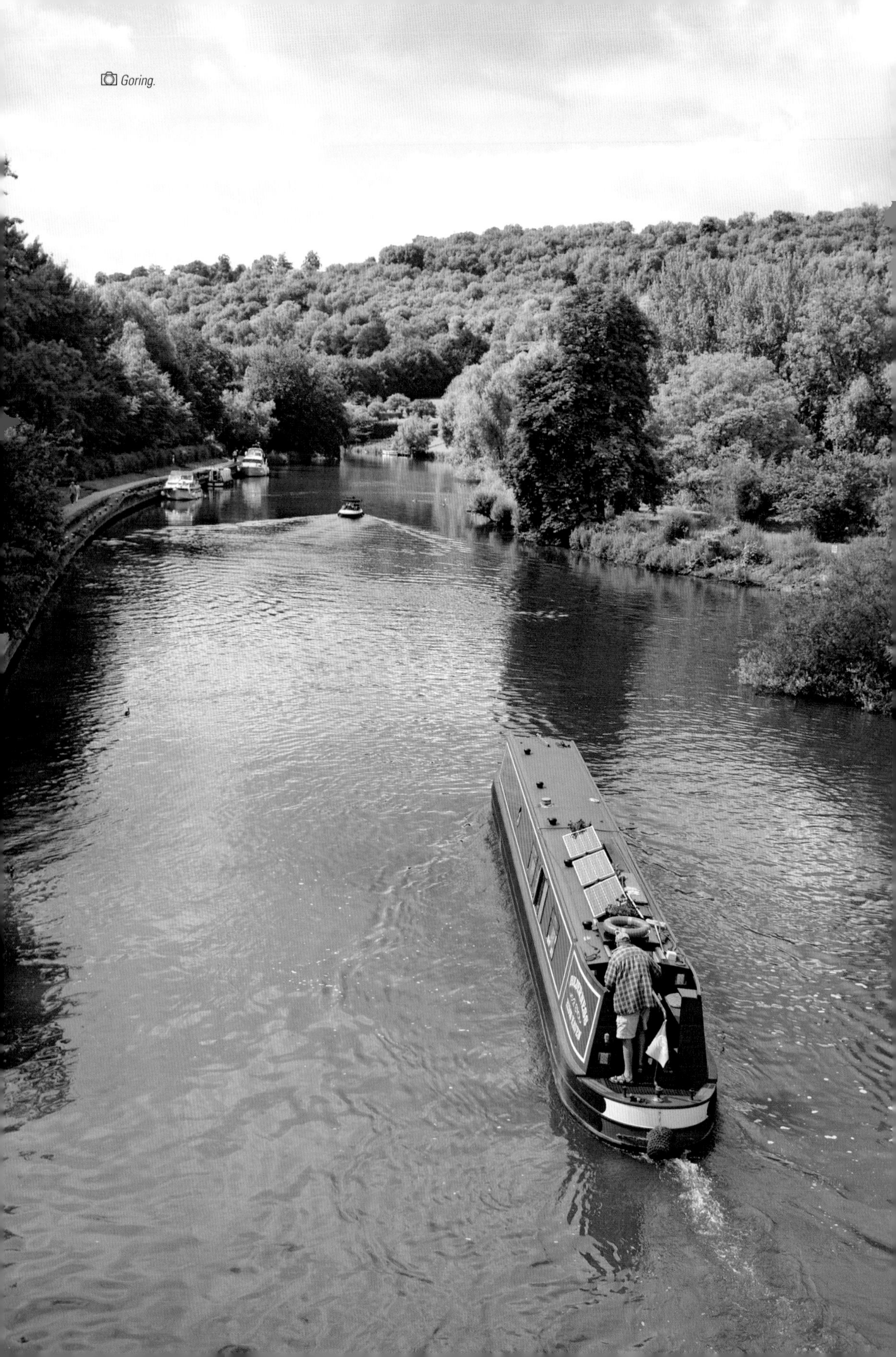

Goring.

Near Moulsford.

Wallingford to Pangbourne

Distance   16.4km

Start   △ Wallingford SU 610 894 / OX10 0BL

Finish   ○ Whitchurch Bridge, Pangbourne SU 636 768 / RG8 7DA

Introduction

Goring Gap is justly celebrated as some of the finest scenery of the whole river. Geoffrey Boumphrey kayaked these waters in the 1930s: *"It is hard to exaggerate the beauty of the miles through the gap to Pangbourne: a hint of downs on the left and then the famous Hartslock Wood, Streatley Hill mounting up to the Berkshire Downs opposite, willows and poplars by the waterside, water lilies and scented rushes breaking the surface."*   Down River 1936

Launch points

Wallingford Bridge SU 610 894 / OX10 0BL – beach on river left downstream of bridge. Car park with barrier at Riverside Park, or park on road outside. Track leading off The Street.

Cholsey SU 601 855 / OX10 9GZ – river right from end of Ferry Lane.

South Stoke SU 594 837 / OX10 9JU – river left from end of Ferry Lane.

Goring Bridge SU 597 808 / RG8 1AU – river left downstream of Goring Lock and beneath bridge. Limited parking nearby on Thames Road.

Whitchurch Bridge SU 636 768 / RG8 7DA – below bridge on river right (Pangbourne side) from Adventure Dolphin car park. Whitchurch Road.

Wallingford

Castle (ruins)

△ 20

△ 21

A4074

A4130

A4130

A4130

A4074

N

North Moreton

South Moreton

Aston Upthorpe

Cholsey

A329

River Thames

Nuffield

To Henley-on-T

A4130

Stoke Row

To Blewbury

A417

B4009

Moulsford Eyots

Moulsford

North Stoke

South Stoke

A4074

Checkendon

Woodcote

Cleeve

Cleeve Eyots

Swann Eyot

Goring

Streatley

Heart Eyot

Goring

B4526

B471

A4074

YHA 22

Grim's Ditch Eyots

The Grotto (mansion)

Gatehampton Eyot

A329

Gatehampton Manor

Beale Wildlife Park

Basildon House

Aldworth

B4009

Whitchurch Hill

Hartslock Aits

B471

Whitchurch-on-Thames

Hardwick House

River Thames

Hardwick Ait

Mapledurham

Whitchurch Mill Ait

Basildon Park

Upper Basildon

Whitchurch

Whitchurch Lock Island

Pangbourne

A329

Mapledurham

Mapledurham Lock Island

Mapledurham Eyot

△ 23

Ferry Eyot

Ashampstead

Tidmarsh

A340

Purley on Thames

Roebuck Ait

Poplar Island

Apr

To Read

Yattendon

0   1   2km

M4

M4

Bradfield

📷 *Below Wallingford.*

Description

Downstream of Wallingford Bridge on river left is Wallingford Meadow, while for 800m the town clings to the river right bank. After the A4130 Wallingford Bypass Bridge (aka Winterbrook Bridge), you are back out in the countryside, with occasional villages skirting the banks. The wooden boathouse on river left was designed by Sir Basil Spence (also responsible for Coventry Cathedral).

The river bores a straight path south, through quiet meadows. You may meet rowing eights around the impressive boathouse of Oxford Brookes Rowing Club, passed on river right. The tower of St Mary's Church in North Stoke is visible, 300m away on the left. Consider a walk to view its fourteenth-century wall paintings. The river bends and braids past Cholsey

Marsh nature reserve on river right, a good place to enjoy Lodden lilies in springtime. The appearance of a road access on river right is a bit of a surprise; this is the site of an old ferry. A few more bends bring you to Moulsford Eyots, several uninhabited islands draped with willows and allegedly haunted! Happy minutes can be wasted playing hide and seek around the overgrown channels, unless of course you are a grown-up and above such things. Directly below, Moulsford Railway Bridge slashes diagonally above the river via two pairs of arches. This viaduct showcases Brunel's groundbreaking engineering; during construction in 1839 (later widened in 1892), he calculated how to construct the spacious arches using only red bricks.

📷 Cleeve Lock.

The gardens of the (affluent) village of Moulsford appear on river right. Paddlers with children mustn't miss the inlet leading to the splendid Sheridan Marine Chandlery, which sells ice cream and pirate flags. Shortly after are the Beetle and Wedge Pub (where H.G. Wells wrote *The History of Mr Polly*) and the remarkable 'Egyptian House', a modern mansion

📷 Chandlers at Moulsford.

made to look ... well, you get the idea.

After Moulsford, the river right bank becomes Berkshire (remaining so until Reading). On river left, reedy Withymead Nature Reserve occupies an island and former boatyard; a few buildings survive. Directly after is the Leatherne Bottel, an historic pub which is now an upmarket gastro-something-or-other. Cleeve Lock marks the start of the Cleeve Eyots, a chain of four islands leading downstream.

"The river expands to a great width, so as to enclose a large island, or rather a chain of islands, which occupies the centre of it, and is clothed with goodly trees."

James Thorne, *Rambles by Rivers* 1849

The lock island is connected by a weir to Cleeve Island, which formerly belonged to Pete Townshend from *The Who*. Another weir leads to the next island and the final, largest island stands alone, disconnected and uninhabited.

At the narrowest part of Goring Gap, the town of Goring and village of Streatley infringe upon on the east and west banks respectively, but these are attractive dwellings. Five hundred metres after the Cleeve Eyots, the river divides around Swann Eyot, which is spanned by Goring Bridge.

"A long and picturesque bridge, from which a fine view is commanded of the river, with its graceful windings and its pretty aits above and below."

Mr and Mrs S.C. Hall,
The Book of the River Thames 1859

The bridge gained concrete innards in 1923, with the appearance of its 1837 wooden predecessor preserved. This is a significant spot; people have crossed the Thames here for millennia, this being the meeting place of the prehistoric Icknield Way and Ridgeway tracks. The Ridgeway National Trail crosses here, following this ancient route.

Swann Eyot belongs to the Swan Hotel, located on the river right side of the island. Its name comes from the family who operated the ferry in the eighteenth century. Moored alongside the hotel is the ornate Magdalen College Barge, last survivor of the Oxford college barges, now used for functions. Be careful exploring this side of the island, as the weir is below. In 1674, sixty (!) passengers died after the ferry got dragged in.

[◎] *Magdalen College Barge, Goring.*

📷 *Goring Lock.*

Goring Lock is river left of Swann Eyot. Note that an additional river left channel leads under the bridge to a mill, with attendant 'Danger No Canoeing' sign. The lock pound was built from timber in 1787, the shortest on the river. The current lock survives from 1921.

After the bridge, uninhabited Heart Eyot (guess what shape) is located at the end of the weir trailing from Swann Eyot. Children of the '80s may be interested to know that the buildings in front of Goring's church include Mill Cottage, George Michael's former home. Children of the '90s shouldn't feel left out, as Gerri Halliwell ('Ginger Spice') lives opposite, in Streatley.

"All the way between Goring and Reading the river continues to present a succession of beautiful and various prospects."

James Thorne, *Rambles by Rivers* 1849

The view ahead from Goring Bridge really is rather fine; densely wooded hillside plunges sharply towards the river right shore, and all around is greenery. Henceforth the downlands are never far from view. A kilometre past Goring, Grim's Ditch Eyots take their name from a prehistoric earthwork which meets the river close by. It is worth exploring behind these three spindly wooded islands, one of which hides a well-preserved pillbox. On the river right hillside is The Grotto, one of a series of eighteenth-century mansions built to take advantage of this picturesque landscape. Conversely, look out for 'The Boating Pavilion', a modern glass box overhanging the water.

Gatehampton Eyot has a narrow channel to seek out behind it. Just past is Gatehampton Railway Bridge (aka Basildon Bridge), another red-brick Brunel construction. The buildings to the left are Gatehampton Manor, while the thirteenth-century tower visible on river right is St Bartholomew's Church, notable as the burial place of Jethro Tull, deceased 1741.

The Thames is redirected south by the Chilterns which rise from the water on river left. This is Hartslock Wood. This chalky nature reserve sprouts cowslips in spring and orchids in early summer. On the opposite side, you briefly glimpse Basildon House atop the hill, built in 1767 and now a National Trust property. The Hartslock Aits are two islands, the larger having a path through its dense trees. Below on river right are moorings and signs for Beale Park Wildlife Park, a zoo established in 1956.

The Chiltern hillside falls back to make space for the Coombe Park Estate (another mansion), and then the road into Pangbourne joins on the right for the final kilometre. A long weir undulates diagonally across the river; in high water, make sure that you keep left to reach the lock! The weir is overlooked on river right by the Swan Inn. A boathouse beside the weir is where in 1968, Robert Plant and Jimmy Page formed *Led Zeppelin*. The River Pang discharges into the weir pool.

Whitchurch Lock was built in 1787, with a re-build in 1875. It occupies the channel between Whitchurch Mill Ait (river left), and Whitchurch Lock Island (river right). There is a further river left channel leading to Whitchurch Mill, an old brick edifice converted to a house. Behind is the 1858 wooden spire of St Mary's Church. Strewn with aged willows and the hunting ground of numerous herons, these channels and pools really are rather lovely.

The channels converge above Whitchurch Bridge (1902), white iron with an attractive

📷 *Pangbourne.*

latticework parapet. This toll bridge keeps the residents of Whitchurch-on-Thames (river left) and Pangbourne (river right) separate. Take out below on river right.

Incidentally, it was here that Jerome K. Jerome's *Three Men in a Boat* abandoned their boat and retreated to the railway station: "Here's to three men well out of a boat!"

Goring Gap

You won't fail to notice the hills closing in, rising around a hundred metres above the Thames. To the east are the Chilterns and to the west the Berkshire Downs terminate at Lough Down. Before the Anglian Glaciation, these downs formed a continuous chalk barrier, redirecting the Thames north-east. Glaciers dammed the river, forming a lake. Around 425,000 years ago the Thames burst through at Goring, establishing its modern course. No obvious hint of this epic catastrophe survives today, just a bucolic backdrop of rolling green hills.

Mapledurham Mill.

© *Appletree Eyot.*

Pangbourne to Reading

Distance   12.2km

Start   △ Whitchurch Bridge, Pangbourne SU 636 768 / RG8 7DA

Finish   ◎ Wokingham Waterside Centre, Reading SU 736 740 / RG6 1PQ

Introduction

The Goring Gap's lush scenery continues to Reading. Presumably, few paddlers have a float through this town high on their wish list ... yet surprisingly, the Thames remains pleasant and attractive, with past industrial grimness long since gone.

Launch points

Whitchurch Bridge SU 636 768 / RG8 7DA – below bridge on river right (Pangbourne side) from Adventure Dolphin car park. Whitchurch Road. Tilehurst SU 686 746 / RG30 6AY – slipway on river right at end of Scours Lane. Limited parking along road.

Caversham Bridge SU 710 746 / RG1 8BD – from park on river right upstream of bridge, car parks (with height barriers) on Thames Side Promenade.

Wokingham Waterside Centre SU 736 740 / RG6 1PQ – river right from parking area with height barrier. Thames Valley Park Drive.

Description

Below Whitchurch Bridge, you will often encounter youth groups from Adventure Dolphin, across the meadow on river right. The meadows continue for three kilometres to Mapledurham Lock, with the Chilterns forming

a shapely backdrop on river left. The first landmark(?) of note is the alpaca farm on river left; the banks are lined with over 800 of the hairy things. After two kilometres, an avenue of trees leads uphill on river left to Hardwick House. This estate originates from the Norman Conquest, but the mansion is mostly Tudor. Elizabeth I and Charles I both visited, the latter to play bowls on day release, while a prisoner. Hardwick Ait is a tiny islet, several gnarled

Hardwick House.

trees clinging to mid river. The Thames then widens upstream of Mapledurham Lock. The pound lock originated in 1777, was enlarged in 1908, and in 1956 became the first on the river to be mechanised. There is a no-frills café beside the lock. On the far side of Mapledurham Lock Island, a long weir links to Mapledurham Eyot; well worth visiting after passing through the lock. There has been a weir and mill hereabouts since at least the Domesday Book (1086). The river left channel leads upstream to wooden Mapledurham Mill, which has (remarkably) been grinding flour since the fifteenth century.

"The view of the old mill at Mapledurham (the most picturesque on the river) ... forms one of the most tranquil scenes that it is possible to imagine, and needs nothing to add to its beauty and harmony." Henry Taunt, *A New Map of the River Thames* 1871

📷 Mapledurham Lock.

The mill was restored in the '80s and has had an Archimedes Screw added. It also features on the cover of a *Black Sabbath* album! Alongside is the red-brick church tower and Mapledurham House, built in 1588 and continuously the residence of the Blount Family. The village and mill were invaded by Nazis in the movie *The Eagle has Landed*.

It is a shame to leave such a wonderful spot, but the Thames now passes wooded Ferry Eyot and skirts Purley, an outlier of Reading.

"Between Purley and Reading ... the scenery is greatly varied, and especially for the first three miles, very beautiful. The islands are ... an extremely pleasing feature in the landscape."

James Thorne, *Rambles by Rivers* 1849

Reading has expanded somewhat since Thorne floated through, but what he described is still recognisable. The river left bank remains meadows. The railway joins the river right bank after a marina (with the conurbation of Tilehurst behind), but there is still a green tree-lined corridor right into the heart of Reading. One mystery is the red post box built into the riverbank beneath the railway ... we have no clue. The islands include Roebuck Ait and a kilometre downstream, the lovely Poplar Island and Appletree Eyot. A century ago they were one long island.

📷 Mapledurham church.

📷 *Purley on Thames.*

The river bends left at a boatyard, leaving the railway. Both banks are now Berkshire until after Caversham, when river left returns to Oxfordshire. There are some posh residences to sneak a look at behind St Mary's Island, and then the river left bank meets Caversham's 'Millionaire's Row', a procession of quirky and desirable townhouses. These finish near the clubhouse of Reading Canoe Club, where you will usually meet slalom or marathon paddlers training. The river right bank is parkland, the Thames Side Promenade.

Caversham Bridge's two boring arches were a big deal when opened in 1926; it was the longest yet made from concrete. Pipers Island extends downstream of the bridge, named after a nineteenth-century ferryman who refused to demolish his house to make way for bridge construction; it was eventually moved (in its 150-ton entirety) on jacks! The island is now smothered by a soulless glass restaurant.

Fry's Island is also named for a nineteenth-century owner. It's also called Montford Island, being the site of an 1163 duel (witnessed by Henry II) between Simon de Montford and a knight accused of cowardice in battle. Directly below is the Thames' newest footbridge, Christchurch Bridge, opened September 2015. It's 120m long and supported by a 50-tonne mast standing 39m above river level. The locals could have saved themselves £20 million, as Reading Bridge is 200m downstream. Built in 1923, the concrete arch was designed tall enough for steamer funnels to pass beneath.

"The river is dirty and dismal here. One does not linger in the neighbourhood of Reading."

Jerome K. Jerome,
Three Men in a Boat 1889

PANGBOURNE TO READING

📷 *Reading houseboat.*

an urban wasteland, but is now a sculpture park and green space. Heron Island follows, covered with housing (no herons).

There is a marked change of character now. Buildings are hidden from sight and the Thames widens as it flows out of town, with dishevelled houseboats lining the banks. One oddity is a mooring on river right signposted for a Tesco Extra. The River Kennet enters on river right under Horseshoe Bridge; Devizes to Westminster racers will know this spot well! Just upstream, Blake's Lock on the Kennet is (confusingly) administered as a Thames Lock by the Environment Agency. The river runs alongside the Kennet and Avon Canal, opened in 1810 and restored in the 1980s. This links to Bristol ... should you need to cross the country.

The Reading that Jerome winced at no longer exists. Here in the centre, the river is clean and the banks are all parks and pleasant walkways. Industry is gone (or at least, well camouflaged) and once Caversham Lock is passed, both banks soon become open spaces again. Caversham Lock is alongside De Bohun Island, which is connected by weir to View Island. The latter was until recently

The sight of broad and (seemingly) endless Dreadnought Reach stretching ahead between open banks is a satisfying change after the brief urban stretch. The lone building on river right is Thames Valley Park Rowing Club, followed by the park itself. The large building fronting the water shortly after is Wokingham Waterside Centre, best known by paddlers for the Marsport shop located on site.

Toad Hall

Fans of Kenneth Grahame's *The Wind in the Willows* will feel a sense of déjà vu; E. H. Shepard's classic illustrations were based upon the area around Pangbourne. For Toad Hall, Shepard clearly took inspiration from both Hardwick and Mapledurham

Houses. The book was written at Cookham, but Grahame lived at Church Cottage in Pangbourne until his death in 1932. Grahame's own inspiration for Toad Hall has been debated, a strong contender being Henley's Fawley Court.

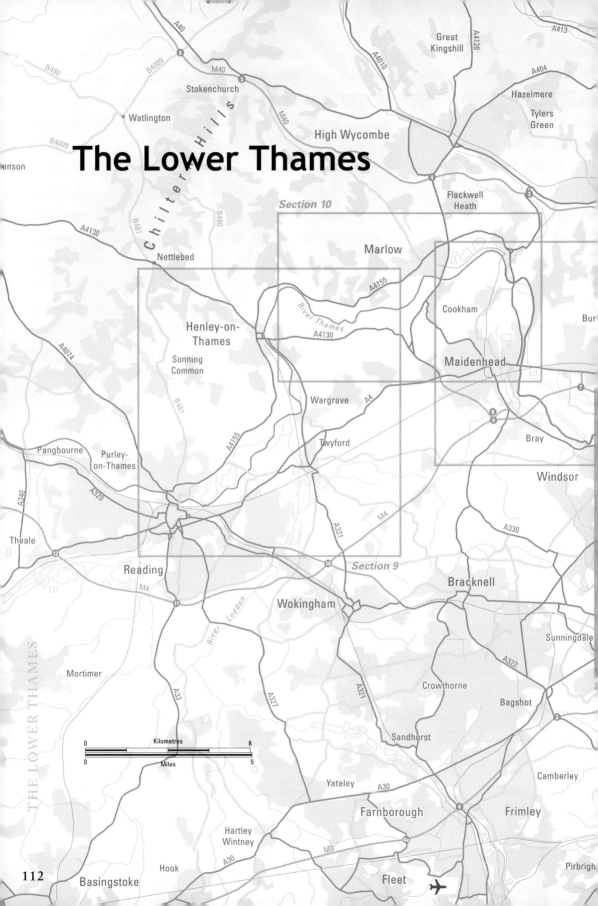

The Lower Thames

Section 10

Section 9

Chiltern Hills

Stokenchurch

Watlington

High Wycombe

Great
Kingshill

Hazelmere

Tylers
Green

Flackwell
Heath

Marlow

Nettlebed

River Thames

A4130

Cookham

Bur

Henley-on-
Thames

Maidenhead

Sonning
Common

Wargrave

A4

Bray

Twyford

Windsor

Pangbourne

Purley-
on-Thames

Theale

M4

Reading

Wokingham

Bracknell

Mortimer

River Loddon

Sunningdale

Crowthorne

Bagshot

Sandhurst

Kilometres

Yateley

Camberley

Farnborough

Frimley

Hartley
Wintney

Hook

Pirbrigh

Basingstoke

Fleet

Temple Island.

Reading to Aston

Distance   17.5km

Start   △ Wokingham Waterside Centre, Reading SU 736 740 / RG6 1PQ

Finish   ○ Aston SU 787 845 / RG9 3DH

Introduction

Below Reading, the Thames enjoys one of its most attractive stretches, punctuated by some idyllic locks, islands and back channels. With Henley-on-Thames on the route, you're also going to experience some posh culture and outlandish wealth.

Launch points

Wokingham Waterside Centre SU 736 740 / RG6 1PQ – river right from parking area with height barrier. Thames Valley Park Drive.

Wargrave SU 786 790 / RG10 8HZ – river right from small picnic area, into back channel beside Lashbrook Ait. Park in small lay-by beside A321 Wargrave Road.

Marsh Lock SU 772 818 / RG9 3HY – river left from Marsh Meadows. Car park is 150m from river on Mill Lane.

Henley SU 767 821 / RG9 1BF – river left from Mill Meadows car park, in front of River and Rowing Museum. Meadow Road. Also, 700m downstream is a public slipway SU 763 828 / RG9 2LJ on river left, junction of A4130 New Street and Wharfe Lane.

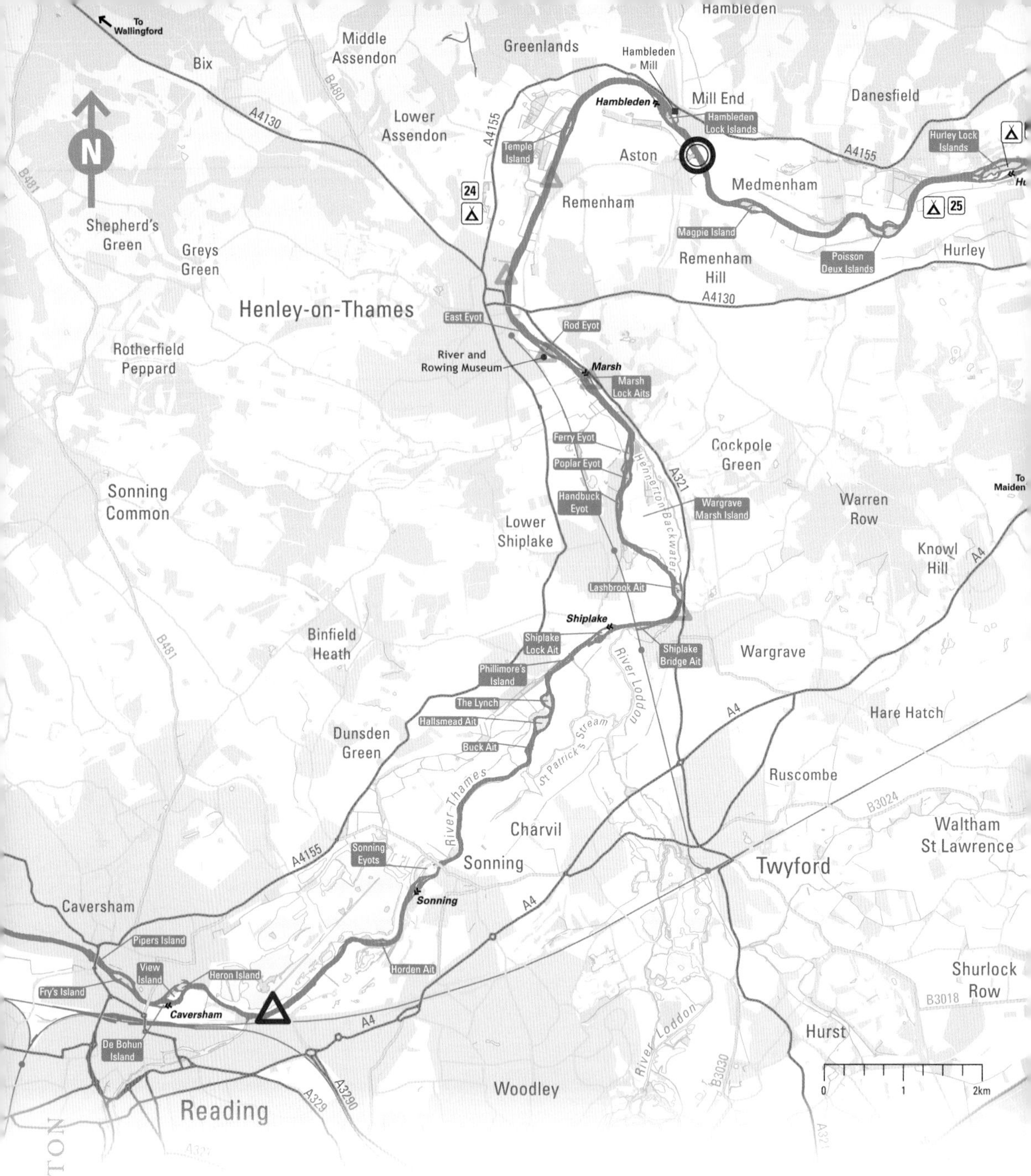

Map labels (as they appear):

To Wallingford · Bix · Middle Assendon · Greenlands · Hambleden · Hambleden Mill · Mill End · Danesfield · A4130 · B480 · Lower Assendon · A4155 · Temple Island · Hambleden · Aston · Hambleden Lock Islands · Hurley Lock Islands · Shepherd's Green · Greys Green · 24 · Remenham · Medmenham · A4155 · 25 · Hurley · Henley-on-Thames · East Eyot · Rod Eyot · Magpie Island · Remenham Hill · A4130 · Poisson Deux Islands · Rotherfield Peppard · River and Rowing Museum · Marsh · Marsh Lock Aits · Cockpole Green · To Maiden · Warren Row · Sonning Common · Ferry Eyot · Poplar Eyot · Handbuck Eyot · Lower Shiplake · A321 · Wargrave Marsh Island · Knowl Hill · A4 · Hennerton Backwater · Lashbrook Ait · River Loddon · Shiplake · Binfield Heath · B481 · Shiplake Lock Ait · Shiplake Bridge Ait · Wargrave · Hare Hatch · Phillimore's Island · The Lynch · Hallsmead Ait · St Patrick's Stream · A4 · Ruscombe · Buck Ait · Dunsden Green · River Thames · B3024 · Waltham St Lawrence · Charvil · Twyford · A4155 · Sonning Eyots · Sonning · A4 · Caversham · Shurlock Row · Pipers Island · B3018 · View Island · Heron Island · Horden Ait · Fry's Island · River Loddon · Hurst · De Bohun Island · A4 · A329 · B3030 · Reading · A3290 · Woodley · 0 1 2km

Remenham SU 770 843 / RG9 3DB – river right, follow footpath 120m to river from limited parking beside church (not Sunday morning). Church Lane.

Aston SU 787 845 / RG9 3DH – parking area on river right at end of Ferry Lane. Also possible on the opposite bank, limited parking however.

📷 *Sonning Bridge.*

Dreadnought Reach runs wide and straight for a kilometre past Thames Valley Park. Early on, the entrance to Thames and Kennet Marina is passed on river left; this also accesses the Caversham Lakes, reclaimed gravel pits where the Olympic rowing squad trains. After an island is passed, Thames Valley Park Nature Reserve is on river right, with meadows and ponds. Amazingly, until its demolition in the 1980s, this was Reading Power Station's coal ash dumping ground.

Horden Ait is uninhabited, although the author recently spotted an intriguing 'Robinson Crusoe' shelter on it. Above the following left bend is nineteenth-century Holme Park Mansion, now a school.

The tower of St Andrew's Church on river right is visible as you approach Sonning Lock, first built in 1773. Below, the Sonning Eyots lead to Sonning Bridge. Jerome reckoned this "the most fairy-like little Nook on the whole river" (*Three Men in a Boat*, 1889) and he may have had a point. The willow-shrouded bridge has eleven quirkily irregular red-brick arches, dating from 1775. The channels converging below the bridge reward exploration; eighteenth-century Sonning Mill (a theatre since 1982) spans the central channel, the river right island shields George Clooney's mansion, and the river left channel flows past the French Horn Restaurant, a nineteenth-century inn. The huge White House-inspired mansion just past the bridge belonged to Uri Geller until 2015. It sold for £15 million; spoon-bending must pay well. Other Sonning residents include Prime Minister Theresa May.

"The river up to Sonning winds in and out through many islands, and is very placid, hushed and lonely."
Jerome K. Jerome,
Three Men in a Boat 1889

Jerome's description of the following kilometres is still spot on after thirteen decades. There is little to interrupt your peace until Shiplake Lock, so drift along and enjoy the ducks, coots and grebes splashing around among the reeds. St Patrick's Stream on river right offers an even quieter diversion, but would mean missing some interesting islands; Buck Ait is tiny, named for the eel traps which were located here. Hallsmead Ait and The Lynch are large and wooded, with paths to investigate and good picnic potential.

The Church of St Peter and Paul (where Tennyson was married in 1850) sits atop a 30m-high chalk scarp forcing the Thames into a right bend. In front is Shiplake College. Directly after, Shiplake House belonged to nineteenth-century politician and friend of Gladstone, Sir Robert Phillimore. It overlooks wooded Phillimore's Island.

Shiplake Lock Ait has been the site of a weir since before 1066, although a pound lock (known as Cotterill's Lock) was first built here in 1773. The island has fixed 'glamping' tents, not a bad spot to be marooned. Downstream, the River Lodden joins from the right. Nestling beneath grim Shiplake Railway Bridge is grassy Shiplake Bridge Ait. Behind is the tower of St Mary's Church, burned down by suffragettes in 1914 in a case of mistaken identity; their target was likely a different church.

You've reached Wargrave, a string of exclusive properties which line the river right bank around a long left bend. In August, the Wargrave and Shiplake Regatta is held here, the biggest after Henley but a rather less formal affair. The St George and Dragon pub has been serving river users since the nineteenth century; why spoil a tradition? The channel behind Lashbrook Ait leads to a launch spot and also to Hennerton Backwater, which passes behind Wargrave Marsh Island.

If you stick with the main channel, a string of uninhabited wooded islands stretches over the next kilometre; Handbuck Eyot, Poplar Eyot and Ferry Eyot, so-named as the Bolney Ferry was historically hereabouts. Behind Ferry Eyot, look for the garden with a narrow gauge railway chugging around it!

Hennerton Backwater rejoins as the river reaches a ridge of chalk hills on river right, re-directing the river north-west towards Henley. Atop the ridge is eighteenth-century Park Place, built as a residence for the future George IV, bought in 2011 for £140 million by a Russian oligarch dissident; the most expensive UK house sale ever.

Shiplake Lock.

📷 *Hennerton Backwater.*

Marsh Lock is recognisable by the long wooden walkway extending out into the middle of the river. There has been a weir here since the fifteenth century, but the first pound lock was constructed in 1773, and the current lock in 1914. Shortly below is Rod Eyot, a long island covered with wooden chalets raised on stilts. You're now in Henley, and the river left park contains the River and Rowing Museum, built in 1998 in a style recalling wooden Thames mills; well worth a visit. East Eyot (aka Bird Island) is a long screen of trees in mid river, and then Henley Bridge is reached. This was built in 1786 in the classical style, with Anne Damer's sculptures on the keystones; a female representing Isis facing upstream, and Old Father Thames facing downstream. At the river left end is fourteenth-century St Mary's church, fronted by two historic pubs; the Angel on the

Bridge and the Red Lion. Below the bridge on river right is Leander Rowing Club, the world's oldest. It was founded in 1897 and celebrated its 101st birthday by letting women join.

Henley Reach stretches straight ahead for two kilometres, allegedly the longest natural straight in Britain. This is possibly the busiest part of the non-tidal river, with all manner of powered and unpowered craft promenading up and down. It all peaks in Regatta week, described by Charles Dickens.

"The river is so inconveniently crowded with steam launches, houseboats, skiffs, gigs, punts, dinghies, canoes and every other conceivable and inconceivable variety of craft."

Dictionary of the Thames 1887

Along Henley Reach, the river left bank changes from Oxfordshire to Buckinghamshire and shortly after is Fawley Court; this 1684

📷 *Henley Bridge.*

Wren-designed mansion is obscured from view, but is the most likely inspiration for Toad Hall in *The Wind in the Willows*. Opposite is the hamlet of Remenham with its thirteenth century church, a pleasant picnic spot.

Henley Reach culminates at Temple Island (aka Regatta Island), fronted by Fawley Temple. This folly was built in 1771 as a fishing lodge for Fawley Court, the first Etruscan-style architecture in the UK. The temple was recently restored after wealthy donors bought a 999-year lease on the island for the regatta. Landing is forbidden without permission, but nobody seems to have told the huge flocks of brent geese roosting hereabouts.

The Thames is coaxed back to a southerly direction by the beech wood-covered Chilterns. The river right bank arcs along Temple Meadow, an SSSI backed by Remenham Hill. The 1850's Italianate house on the left is Greenlands, now the home of Henley Business School (University of Reading) but notable as the subject of Jerome K. Jerome's driest joke. In *Three Men in a Boat*, he briefly mentioned it: "The rather uninteresting residence of my newsagent". Most readers won't have been aware who lived there; a certain W.H. Smith.

Hambleden Lock might be the most picturesque on the entire river. Opened in 1773, a weir and mill had already been here since the Domesday Book. The mill has traces from the sixteenth century, and worked until 1952. This huge white wood edifice has been sympathetically converted to flats. Pottering around the Hambleden Lock Islands below

□ *Hambleden Mill.*

the weir rewards the paddler with some great vistas recalling a bygone Thames. It's tough to tear yourself away and paddle the last few hundred metres to Aston.

Refreshment can be found 400m up Ferry Lane at the Flower Pot pub. Red kites roost in the trees along the lane.

Variations

Aristocratic canoeist Eleanor Barnes recommended "The swift water of St Patrick with its banks of buttercups" (*As the Water Flows* 1920). **St Patrick's Stream** has a steady flow as it bypasses the 1.5m fall of Shiplake Lock. Enter past the 'unsuitable for navigation' sign to explore a hidden world bounded by reeds and weeping willows, with the occasional branch to dodge. After 1.5km, a side channel leads upstream to a small weir and after 2km the River Lodden is joined, leading past private gardens to the Thames in another 1.3km. Look out for fritillaries on the riverside meadows and of course, the Lodden lily. The Stream is popular with anglers, stay alert and try not to surprise them.

Henley Royal Regatta

Henley Royal Regatta runs for five days in early July, a key part of 'The Season' where privileged Britons perform mating rituals involving absurd clothing and champagne quaffing. The first Oxford and Cambridge Boat Race was held on Henley Reach in 1829 and Henley's annual Regatta began in 1839. It became 'Royal' after Prince Albert attended in 1851.

During Regatta week, the river right bank is obscured by marquees and spectator seating and the river itself is jam-packed with craft. Races start at Temple Island. The river is kept open to passing traffic, but you will be directed well clear of the regatta course.

Hennerton Backwater makes for a similarly lovely diversion, maintained and kept clear by the Hennerton Backwater Association. The entrance is beneath a tiny duckable bridge behind Willow Marina. Initially the channel squeezes so intimately through rather nice gardens that you suspect you've made a mistake. However, most of the two kilometres are a delight, with silent greenery interrupted only by the blue-orange flash of the kingfisher.

A 'figure of eight' paddle from Wargrave taking in St Patrick's Stream, Hennerton Backwater and the main river is highly recommended!

© Winter Hill.

Aston to Cookham

Distance	14.8km
Start	△ Aston SU 787 845 / RG9 3DH
Finish	○ Cookham Bridge SU 898 855 / SL6 9SW

Introduction

If there is such a thing as quintessentially Thames, this section is it. The river is the common thread tying together this attractive landscape's appealing history and culture.

Launch points

Aston SU 787 845 / RG9 3DH – parking area on river right at end of Ferry Lane. Also possible on the opposite bank, limited parking however.
Medmenham SU 806 837 / SL7 2ER – river left from small parking area at end of Ferry Lane.
Marlow SU 852 862 / SL7 1NQ – slipway on river left at end of St Peter Street. Limited parking nearby.

Bourne End SU 884 873 / SL8 5PS – river left, car park with height barrier 200m away across railway, on Coldmoorholme Lane.
Cookham Bridge SU 898 855 / SL6 9SW – slipway on river right after bridge, beside Ferry Inn. Limited parking spaces. End of Ferry Lane.

Description

"From Medmenham to sweet Hambledon Lock the river is full of peaceful beauty."

Jerome K. Jerome,
Three Men in a Boat 1889

In the eight kilometres to the town of Marlow, the Thames wiggles through lovely country-side, with constant interest along the banks.

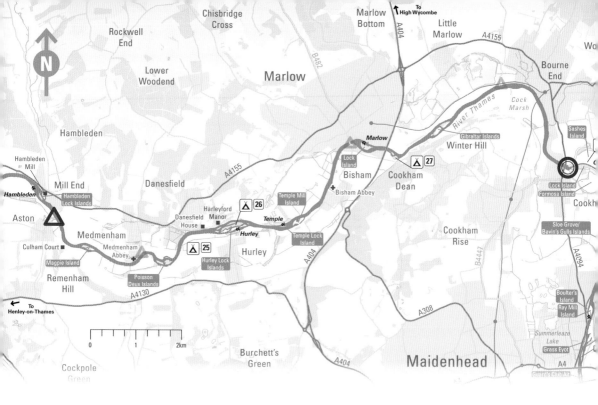

The first landmark is Culham Court on river right, a 1770 mansion amidst landscaped parkland where white deer roam. The Swiss billionaire who bought this in 2007 also bought Hambleden village at the same time, presumably with the leftover change. The estate overlooks Magpie Island, a large wooded nature reserve with various channels to delve into.

The white building with a tower which appears rather suddenly on river left is twelfth-century Medmenham Abbey.

"… it acquired great notoriety as the meeting place of the club of debauches … of their doings it would be unwise to speak, but the motto over the doorway sufficiently shows the class of men."

Henry Taunt,

A New Map of the River Thames 1871

The motto which Taunt recoiled from is Fay ce que voudras – 'do whatever you want'.

This former monastery was leased in 1751 by Chancellor of the Exchequer Sir Francis Dashwood, for his Hellfire Club meetings. These were drunken pagan orgies, not a phrase you hear much in canoeing guidebooks. Among other unorthodox practices, club members released a baboon dressed as Satan into a service at Medmenham's Church, causing the congregation to flee in terror.

The Poisson Deux Islands take their name from a medieval fish weir, but are also known as the Frogmill or Black Boy Islands, the latter apparently a reference to the dark complexion of Charles II. Landing to explore and picnic is possible, however avoid disturbing nesting wildfowl. Shortly after, beside Frogmill Farm on river right, the ice cream barge is often moored; it's exactly what it sounds like!

Uphill on river left, the white mansion is

📷 *Hurley Lock.*

Danesfield House (a hotel since 1991), overlooking Hurley Weir. The weir arcs in several stages around the seven Hurley Lock Islands, a rewarding area to explore.

"I could stay a month without having sufficient time to drink in all the beauty of the scene."

Jerome K. Jerome,
Three Men in a Boat 1889

In spring, the islands are covered with Lodden lilies. Camping is possible by the lock, and also Camping Island has fixed tents, the original campers having arrived for respite from the London Blitz. Hurley Lock was a flash lock known as Newlock in the sixteenth century; a timber winch used to haul boats through still survives. The pound lock was first built in 1773, in conjunction with pound locks at Temple and Marlow. There is a café just below the lock, opposite Freebody's Boatyard;

this family have been involved in Thames boats since the thirteenth century and their boatbuilding company is over three hundred years old. On the far river left shore behind the islands is red-brick Harleyford Manor (1755), nowadays a marina and holiday resort. Adjacent is Charger's Paddock, so named as a former resident fought at Waterloo and kept his regiment's horses here.

"No house on the river has a sweeter situation; here are cannonballs and fortifications (against whom intended I do not know), neatly kept landing places, the usual trespassers' boards, and some lovely backwaters."

George D Leslie, *Our River* 1888

Hurley village is reached by a path from the river right lock channel. The village is on the site of a priory and later mansion where in 1688, nobles plotted the so-called Glorious Revolution.

The next lock is less than a kilometre downstream. Wooden Temple Footbridge spans the river above Temple Lock. The name comes from the Templar Knights who ran a mill hereabouts. In the late nineteenth and early twentieth centuries, three children of lock keepers tragically drowned here.

The river flows through the estate of the former Bisham Abbey; the surviving buildings on river right are now the National Sports Centre. You will see elite athletes training in the gardens, possibly also the England football team whose HQ this is. After the Dissolution of the Monasteries, Bisham was given by Henry VIII to Anne of Cleves, who passed it to the Hoby family. Elizabeth I visited as a youngster. Her acquaintance Lady Elizabeth Hoby beat or starved her son to death, allegedly for blotting

his copybook; this appalling lady's tomb is in adjacent Bisham Church. This lovely building's twelfth-century pointed tower opens directly onto the river front.

Opposite the church on river left is Bondig Bank, a small River Thames Society reserve where alder and willow branches drape across the river.

The river now passes Marlow, unmistakeable by its suspension bridge and the tall spire of All Saints Church at the river left end. Marlow Bridge is the only suspension bridge on the non-tidal river. Opened in 1832, it was designed by William Tierney Clark, also responsible for Hammersmith Bridge in London. Jerome K. Jerome wrote *Three Men in a Boat* in Marlow at the Two Brewers Inn, describing it as "One of the pleasantest river centres I know of … there is lovely country around it, too". Other notable residents have included Percy and Mary Shelley (*Frankenstein* was written here), poet T.S. Eliot and rower Sir Steve Redgrave. The latter's incredible feat of five gold medals in five successive Olympics is honoured by a statue in the Riverside Gardens on river left above the bridge.

"Who ate puppy-pie under Marlow Bridge?" was a local taunt to passing bargemen; apparently bargemen had helped themselves to a riverside inn's food too often, so the innkeeper baked dog excrement into a pie and left it on the windowsill to be stolen …

Marlow Lock dates from 1927. It is hemmed in by exclusive-yet-ugly housing, but boasts a great view back upstream to the weir and bridge. An unnamed island leads under the A404 By-pass Bridge, where the river bends sharply left beneath the wooded slopes of Winter Hill. On the right is Longridge Outdoor Activity Centre, with young people usually out on the water in paddlecraft. The river follows the base of the hill, the shore lined by some impressive properties. Behind are the beeches of Quarry Wood, undoubtedly the inspiration for *The Wind in the Willows*' Wild Wood ("We don't go there very much, we river-bankers"); atop Winter Hill is Cookham Dean, where Kenneth Grahame wrote the book.

The Gibraltar Islands are two islands, the first hosting several buildings and adjoined to the shore by a footbridge. Beside this bridge on river right is a truly incredible wooden-framed mansion-cottage, which defies description

but is penned in to be this author's first acquisition following a lottery win (or The Revolution, whichever comes first).

The remaining three kilometres to Cookham Bridge see the Thames follow a wide right bend, with Winter Hill falling back from the river's edge to make space for Cock Marsh. This pasture has been continually grazed since the thirteenth century, and the Bronze Age burial mounds (excavated by an archaeologist named Cock, hence the name) show that it is truly ancient. The rare brown galingale (actually brown-purple in colour) grows here. The National Trust has managed large tracts of Cock Marsh and Winter Hill since 1934.

The outside of the bend (river left) is Bourne End, with its only connection across the river to Cock Marsh (and the popular Bounty pub) being a 1993 footbridge alongside Bourne End Railway Bridge. The unsheltered banks make this stretch popular with sailors, and you pass several clubs. The River Wye joins (almost unnoticed) after the bridge; a Chiltern stream not to be confused with the Welsh/English border river.

The right bank is cowslip-studded Cookham Moor, remaining attractive all the way to Cookham Bridge. This 1867 span of blue-painted iron carries the A4094. The Ferry Inn is on river right directly below, with a slipway alongside. After landing, a short stroll to Cookham's Stanley Spencer Gallery is worthwhile to grasp how the painter dramatically reinterpreted his local landscape.

Below Boveney Lock.

Cookham to Windsor

Distance	14.8km
Start	△ Cookham Bridge SU 898 855 / SL6 9SW
Finish	○ Windsor Leisure Centre SU 957 772 / SL4 5HU

Introduction

"Here the scenery is the grandest on the river, but it is impossible to give any adequate description of it: it must be seen."   Henry Taunt, *A New Map of the River Thames* 1871

Cookham to Maidenhead is considered by many to be the most beautiful stretch of the entire Thames. It should be noted that it is popular with other water users. Below Maidenhead, the scenery is less grand but the river much quieter.

Launch points

Cookham Bridge SU 898 855 / SL6 9SW – slipway on river right after bridge, beside Ferry Inn. Limited parking spaces. End of Ferry Lane.

Maidenhead SU 902 819 / SL6 8NJ – river right across A4094 Ray Mead Road from the Riverside Gardens car park. Free parking available close by. Boulter's Lock car park (SU 902 825 / SL6 8JB) 700m upstream on A4094 Lower Cookham Road) is another option, but has a height barrier.

Bray SU 903 797 / SL6 2AU – slipway on river right at end of Ferry Lane, however no parking close by.

Windsor Leisure Centre SU 957 772 / SL4 5HU – river right, between A332 Windsor and Eton By-pass Bridge and Leisure Centre at end of

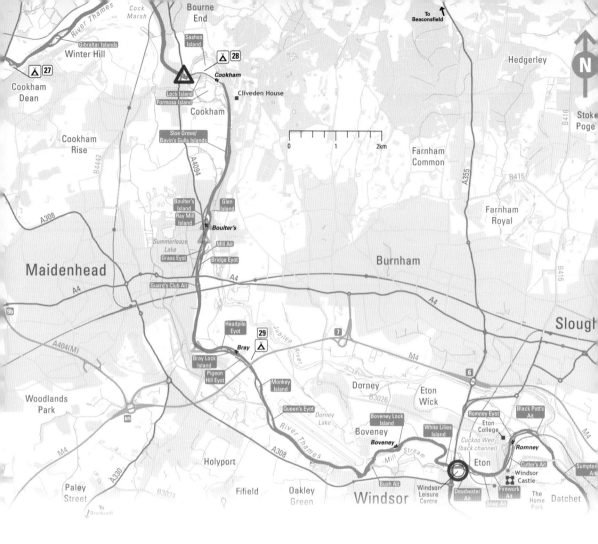

lane leading off Stovell Road. Car parks along lane and around Leisure Centre.

Description

Directly below Cookham Bridge, the Thames splits four ways(!). From river left to right, are:

- Hedsor Water, the original channel, which splits below a weir around a wooded isle before passing Hedsor Wharf (a busy dock before the weir was built).
- Sashes Island (Old English: *Sceaf's Isle*), 9 hectares of farmland where camping is possible.
- Sashes Stream, widened to become the navigation channel when Cookham Lock was built in 1830.
- Lock Island, a narrow wooded strip.
- Odney Weir Stream. The weir is especially dangerous and has sadly claimed the life of a paddler training for the DW Race.
- Formosa Island, 20 hectares, including eighteenth-century Formosa House,

Sashes Stream.

Spring Cottage, Cliveden Reach.

built for Admiral George Young.

• Lulle Brook, a narrow channel leading to a weir.

You will of course first take Sashes Stream to the lock, which is backdropped by wooded hillside; simply stunning. Taking time to then venture back upstream to explore the other channels is recommended.

The various channels converge into Cliveden Reach: "In its unbroken loveliness this is, perhaps, the sweetest stretch of all the river" according to Jerome K. Jerome. The beeches of the Cliveden Estate rise from the river left bank, topped by Cliveden House, which comes into view further downstream. This opulent Italianate mansion, designed by Sir Charles Barry, was completed in 1862. Through the twentieth century it was owned by the extraordinarily wealthy Astor dynasty, whose Octagon Temple mausoleum looms above the river. Nancy Astor was the first woman to take up a seat in the House of Commons (1919) but Cliveden is of course best known for the Profumo Affair; Spring Cottage, the riverside chalet, was rented by Dr Stephen Ward. The estate is now managed by the National Trust. Cliveden House is best seen from Bavin's Gulls Islands (aka Sloe Grove Islands), five narrow isles, the last being Picnic Island (does what it says on the tin). Cliveden Reach is indisputably a beautiful spot, but you are unlikely to enjoy it alone. There is usually traffic of over-large cruisers, seemingly acquired by wealthy Maidenhead residents for the sole purpose of making the three-kilometre round-trip at excessive speeds.

The Profumo Affair

Dr Stephen Ward wheedled himself into high society by acting as a pimp to the glitterati, organising hedonistic parties at Cliveden. It emerged in 1963 that Minister of War John Profumo had been doing inappropriate things with nineteen year-old Christine Keeler in Cliveden's outdoor swimming pool. She was also involved with the Soviet Naval Attaché! The resulting scandal helped bring down the Conservative government. Ward committed suicide.

The passage through Maidenhead's suburbs, with artificially high banks on river right, sharply contrasts Cliveden Reach. After being made accessible by the railway, the town exploded along the river as a holiday resort. The upmarket villas at the town's upstream end were built for wealthy newcomers.

The café, gardens, and ice cream-clutching crowds around Boulter's Lock echo the Victorian and Edwardian mania for boating here (over a thousand small boats passed daily!). Boulter's Lock drops 2.39m, second only to Teddington on the Lower Thames. The deep pound and its jostling traffic were immortalised in Edward Gregory's 1895 painting *Boulter's Lock, Sunday Afternoon*. Incidentally, a 'boulter' was a miller.

Boulter's Lock.

At least seven islands lead the paddler through Maidenhead; 1.6km long Glen Island's river left back channel leads off to the artificial Jubilee River. Boulter's Island is connected to the river right bank by Boulter's Lock. Ray Mill Island (named after a past miller) is popular with the public and is connected to Glen Island by Boulter's Weir. Further downstream, Grass Eyot is recognisable for its tall poplars, Mill Ait is tiny, and Bridge Eyot with its houseboats is just upstream of the balustraded arches of Maidenhead Bridge (1772). The final isle is Guard's Club Ait (aka Buck's Ait), a long nature reserve leading beneath Maidenhead Railway Bridge: "Probably the finest brick bridge in England" (James Thorne, *Rambles by Rivers* 1849). The two thirty-nine metre arches of Brunel's 1838 construction for the Great Western Railway are still the longest brick arches in the world. It's known as The Sounding Arch due to the echo within. J.M.W. Turner painted it; *Rain, Speed and Steam* hangs in the National Gallery.

Maidenhead's 'Millionaire's Row' lines the river right bank as far as a left bend, where the thirteenth-century chalk tower of Bray Church indicates that you've left Maidenhead. You're still among absurd wealth; teeny Bray possesses two of Britain's four Michelin three-star restaurants; should you be feeling peckish, Michel Roux Jr's Waterside Inn might find space for you.

Bronze Age artefacts have been retrieved from both Headpile and Pigeon Hill Eyots, long wooded isles above and below Bray Lock and connected by the weir. The latter island

📷 *Exploring Cuckoo Weir back channel.*

is overshadowed by New Thames Bridge, carrying the noisy M4.

While the remainder of this section passes through some of Britain's wealthiest and most exclusive locales, from the water it really is rather peaceful and attractive.

Monkey Island was previously called Monk's Eyot and belonged to Burnham Abbey. The island was augmented by rubble from the Great Fire of London. In the eighteenth century, the Duke of Marlborough added the Fishing Lodge, famous for its ceiling paintings of monkeys doing sports (yes, really). A paddle around doesn't reveal much, but this secretive island (now a plush hotel) was a social hub; 'mad' George III recovered here (with pet monkey), Edward VII picnicked, HG Wells and Elgar hung out. Trivia – the Birmingham Six spent their first night of freedom here.

Queen's Eyot is another exclusive enclave, having belonged to Eton College since 1923. The island and its clubhouse are not even open to students!

Film buffs will enjoy the next bit. In 1951, Hammer Films built Bray Studios right beside the river. The home of Hammer horror movies, from *Curse of Frankenstein* in 1957 to *Mummy's Shroud* in 1966, is looking dilapidated but is still

📷 *Bray Studios.*

📷 *Oakley Court.*

in use. Directly after is the Gothic façade of Oakley Court, now a hotel. This grotesque 1857 mansion appeared in *Brides of Dracula* (1962) and post-Hammer, *The Rocky Horror Picture Show* (1975). Less frivolously, during WWII this was General de Gaulle's residence and the headquarters of the French Resistance.

Opposite on river left is Eton Dorney, site of the 2012 Olympic rowing events. This 2.2km lake, completed in 2006, is hidden from view behind a nature reserve which – should you fancy a leg stretch – can be accessed from the mooring spot at SU 937 774.

Bush Ait marks the point where Mill Stream leaves on river right to pass south of Windsor Race Course. Continuing on the main channel, to the north of the race course, you experience a peaceful enclave. The isolated timber tower of the twelfth-century Church of St Mary Magdalene rears above the river atop a river left mound. It closed in 1975, but a notice board indicates where you can access the key. Boveney Lock (1938) is one of the remoter Thames locks, and then "we catch the first good peep of the Royal Castle of Windsor" (Henry Taunt, *A New Map of the River Thames* 1871); Windsor is imminent. A jungly back channel known as Cuckoo Weir tempts on river left (there is no weir). Most will stick with the main channel approaching the A332 Windsor and Eton By-pass Bridge via tortuous bends past White Lilies Island on river right, home to several exclusive properties (Natalie Imbruglia named an album after it when she lived there). The bridge itself is a lacklustre introduction to Windsor, but the castle behind will divert your attention. Take out directly after the bridge on river right.

Boveney Lock rollers.

Variations

The channels below Cookham Bridge could swallow a day of exploration and picnicking, but first read Chapter 7 of *The Wind in the Willows,* 'The Piper at the Gates of Dawn'. Really, do it! It describes a visit to Hedsor Water, and is sufficiently trippy to have been used by *Pink Floyd* as the title of their first album.

The **Jubilee River** Flood Alleviation Scheme is an 11.6km artificial channel, leading from Boulter's Lock to below Romney Lock. It was completed in 2002, at a cost of £110 million, to protect 10,000 homes (built on the floodplain) from flooding. Now, it is a remarkably lush green corridor of islands and reed beds worth exploring by paddle. Crucially, it's not possible to enter the Jubilee River from its upstream end; the first weir is deadly and unportageable. The remaining four weirs have portage paths but they are neglected and overgrown. Discreetly access the Jubilee River from the A4 Bath Road (SU 905 813 / SL6 0AJ) near Taplow, or consider an out and back trip from Windsor.

Mill Stream leads 2.3km behind Windsor Race Course to the A332 bridge. It is easily navigable to the Racecourse Marina but then becomes narrow with potential tree blockages, and a 300m portage is required on river right past Clewer Mill's weir. Below it is known as Clewer Mill Stream. Explore with care!

At Runnymede.

Windsor to Chertsey

Distance 19.3km

Start △ Windsor Leisure Centre SU 957 772 / SL4 5HU

Finish ○ Chertsey Bridge TQ 054 666 / KT16 8JA

Introduction

If you've driven through the populous suburbs which surround the Thames' entry into London, you'll be amazed by the contrast on the river itself. While expensive property often crowds the banks, nature is firmly ascendant.

Launch points

Windsor Leisure Centre SU 957 772 / SL4 5HU – river right, between A332 Windsor and Eton By-pass Bridge and Leisure Centre at end of lane leading off Stovell Road. Car parks along lane and around leisure centre.

Runnymede SU 997 731 / TW19 5AE – river right from National Trust car park beside A308. Check gate closure times. Also, Runnymede Pleasure Grounds car park TQ 007 724 / TW20 0AD is 1.3km downstream along the A308.

Staines (Church Island) TQ 029 718 / TW18 4XZ – from Lammas Recreational Ground onto the back channel on river left behind Church Island. Limited parking in Church Lane, or use the recreational ground's car park accessed from the B376 Wraysbury Road.

Staines (Truss's Island) TQ 034 699 / TW18 3LS – river right from Truss's Island Car Park, which has a height barrier. A320 Chertsey Lane. Also

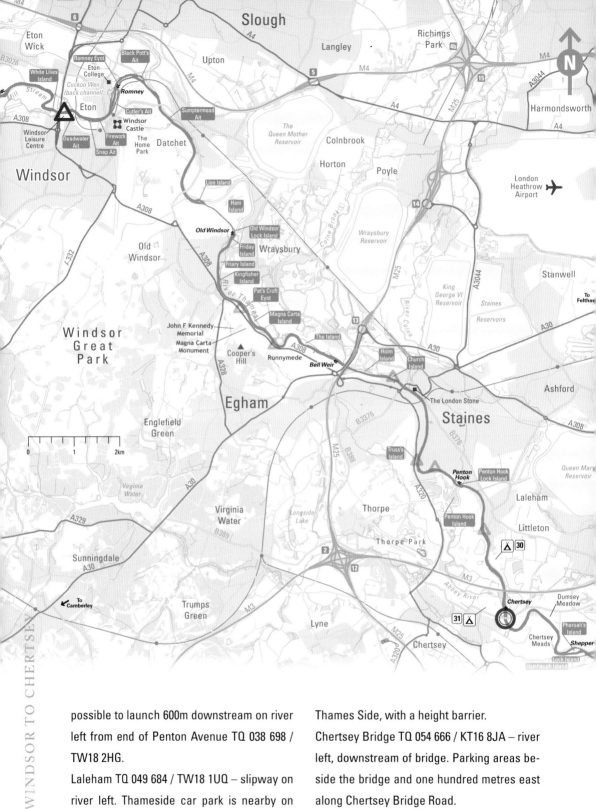

possible to launch 600m downstream on river left from end of Penton Avenue TQ 038 698 / TW18 2HG.

Laleham TQ 049 684 / TW18 1UQ – slipway on river left. Thameside car park is nearby on Thames Side, with a height barrier.

Chertsey Bridge TQ 054 666 / KT16 8JA – river left, downstream of bridge. Parking areas beside the bridge and one hundred metres east along Chertsey Bridge Road.

📷 *Windsor Castle.*

Description

Through Windsor, there is plenty to see! The meadow on river left is The Brocas, owned by Eton College. Windsor Railway Bridge (1849, Brunel) is the oldest wrought iron bridge in use. Beneath is Deadwater Ait, named after the river right back channel but known until the 1930s as Baths Ait; men came here to swim. Snap and Firework Aits follow, the latter so-named as (until 1891, when this event relocated to Romney Eyot), Eton College launched fireworks from here every 4th June, the birthday of their benefactor George III. Dominating the skyline is the long bulk of Windsor Castle, with Edward III's round tower forming the centrepiece. The largest inhabited castle in the world, it has been a royal residence since 1070. In 1917, our Royal family tactfully ditched their surname 'Saxe-Coburg' as too Germanic and adopted the castle's name instead. If the Royal Standard flag is flying, our Queen is at home.

After Windsor Bridge (1822) is passed, the navigation channel directs you river right of Romney Eyot to Romney Lock. This dates from 1797 but was rebuilt in 1980. Romney Eyot is actually two long islands ('The Romneys') with a weir in between, where Isaak Walton (*The Compleat Angler*) fished. Hidden from view are the channels around Cutler's Ait; consider paddling back upstream to explore as they are overlooked by the pinnacled fifteenth-century chapel of Eton College, Britain's most exclusive public school.

"Eton College, that noble seminary of learning, has every advantage from situation which the luxuriant hand of nature could bestow."

Picturesque Views on the River Thames,
Samuel Ireland 1791

📷 *Windsor Home Park.*

Founded in 1440 by Henry VI, Eton has produced nineteen Prime Ministers and continues to be hugely influential. On the nearest Saturday to 4th June, you'll meet a flotilla of students in pretend naval uniforms, knee-breeches and black silk stockings. Try not to laugh.

The river right bank opens out revealing The Home Park, the royal garden. The first kilometre has public access and passes Black Pott's Ait (former site of a fishing weir), crossed by Black Pott's Railway Bridge. The Jubilee River confluence is directly downstream.

Victoria Bridge and Albert Bridge are 2.2 kilometres apart. Both were built for Prince Albert in 1851, replacing a comical effort at Datchet which (due to a funding dispute) was iron at one end, wood at the other. Just after Victoria Bridge, the river left bank is actually Sumptermead Ait. The Home Park is private here; signs along the river right shore remind you of your lowly status. The changing views of castle and parkland are however fantastic. Frogmore House (1680), the birthplace of Lord Louis Mountbatten, is glimpsed before the latter bridge.

One endearing/aggravating quirk is that mid way through The Home Park to Old Windsor Lock is directly under the flight path of Heathrow Airport's two runways. The noise and closeness of jets constantly taking off has to be experienced to be believed, but plane spotters will be in Nirvana.

Lion Island sits above a weir, with the New Cut departing to river right. Dug in 1822, this created Ham Island, now occupied by a bird reserve and sewage works. The approach to Old Windsor Lock through the Cut is lined by raised bungalows, a regular sight henceforth. The natural channel rejoins below the lock at

📷 *Bell Weir Lock.*

Friday Island, allegedly named as it resembles Man Friday's footprint. The island's cottage was home until 1991 to Dr Julius Grant, inventor of Marmite (he didn't like it).

Friary Island is barely discernable, being covered by the suburbs of Wraysbury which continue to Kingfisher Island. The river right bank enters Surrey and a pair of gates (designed

📷 *Magna Carta mural, Bell Weir Lock.*

by Lutyens) alongside Pat's Croft Eyot signify that you have reached Runnymede. If you slept through your history lessons, this lovely spot is where in 1215 'bad' King John was forced to sign the Magna Carta. The lush meadows and wooded Cooper's Hill on river right are managed by the National Trust, and dotted with memorials.

Magna Carta Island has a small back channel; look for overgrown ruins on the island. Behind are the grounds of Ankerwycke Priory, also ruined. *The Three Men in a Boat* moored at 'Picnic Point' hereabouts.

The Island (covered with houses and shielding a willow-strewn back channel) is the only landmark in the approach to Bell Weir Lock, alongside the Runnymede Hotel. The 1868 lock features murals celebrating Magna Carta.

📷 *Holm Island.*

As Colne Brook joins through the vast area of reservoirs on river left, Runnymede Bridge is reached; the M25. Staines' industrial outskirts are hidden behind trees on river right, and can be avoided further by taking Holm Island's long back channel. In the 1930s, Edward VIII used this island's seclusion to woo Wallis Simpson. Church Island's back channel leads past Lammas Recreational Ground, a potential launch spot.

Staines Bridge was designed with three white granite arches by George Rennie in 1832. Joseph Pennell and Elizabeth Robins damned Staines as "The rival of Reading in ugliness" (*The Stream of Pleasure* 1891), which is unfair to both towns. Staines isn't ugly; it's just a bit bland, from the river at least. One point of interest is the replica of The London Stone

on the river left bank below the bridge. From 1285, this marked both the tidal limit and the beginning of the Corporation of London's jurisdiction over the river. London began here! The original is in Staines' Spelthorne Museum. The other interesting thing about Staines is that the railway bridge's yellow stripes are to deter swan strikes.

📷 *The London Stone, Staines.*

A long succession of bungalows leads out of town. Variation is offered by Truss's Island on river right; Charles Truss was an eighteenth-century clerk who designed many of the pound locks. This was an early nature reserve, recovered from waste ground by local volunteers in 1827! There are sculptures, information boards and a picnic area to enjoy. Penton Hook Lock takes its name from the sharp meander it cuts across. This cut of only fifty metres was dug in 1815; boats were already taking the overland shortcut in high water levels. The lock keeper's cottage bears the City Arms, being the highest lock then controlled by the Corporation of London.

The Thames escapes suburbia for the final reach to Chertsey. The village of Laleham is passed on river left, All Saint's Church being the resting place of poet Matthew Arnold. Meadows fronting Laleham Abbey (a nineteenth-century mansion) and Laleham Park are passed before the M3 motorway bridge.

Directly below is Chertsey Lock, reached by a long channel leading along the brink of the weir; be careful in high water!

The seven elegant arches of Chertsey Bridge have kept Surrey and Middlesex apart since 1785. Take out on river left.

Variations

The quiet 1.6km channel around **Ham Island** can be explored from the downstream end.

The natural oxbow forming uninhabited **Penton Hook Island** was utilised in 1665 as a plague burial ground, and is now an Environment Agency-owned nature reserve (popular with fishermen). Look out for parakeets, grebes and voles. The adjacent flooded gravel pits host the huge Penton Hook Marina.

The tiny **Abbey River** leads away to rejoin at Chertsey Lock after about three kilometres. It is overgrown and hard going, re-entering the Thames via a small weir and set of rollers.

Runnymede and Magna Carta

After five days of cross-river negotiations, on 15th June 1215 King John reluctantly signed the Magna Carta. While his barons sought curbed royal power, the 'great charter' has subsequently been celebrated as the origin of legally-backed human rights. It's unclear where it happened; a stone slab erected on Magna Carta Island in the nineteenth century was wishful thinking.

Opposite the island is the 1957 Magna Carta Monument, a gift from American lawyers acknowledging Magna Carta's influence on the US Constitution. The 1965 John F. Kennedy Memorial stands on an acre of land donated to the USA, and high above on Cooper's Hill is the 1953 Commonwealth Air Forces Memorial, honouring 20,456 WWII airmen with no named grave.

Chertsey to Teddington

Distance 20.4km to lock

Start △ Chertsey Bridge TQ 054 666 / KT16 8JA

Finish ○ Teddington TQ 171 714 / TW10 7YE

Introduction

"There are, of course, delightful interludes, but then again villas, banks, kept respectable by smooth cement, and luxury – and launches."

Eleanor Barnes, *As The Water Flows* 1920
The Thames has now passed the tipping point into an urban waterway; the good news is that these surroundings are consistently interesting and that plenty of green spaces survive in the complex waterworld of channels approaching the Tideway.

Launch points

Chertsey Bridge TQ 054 666 / KT16 8JA – river left, downstream of bridge. Parking areas beside the bridge and 100 metres east along Chertsey Bridge Road.

Shepperton Lock TQ 074 659 / TW17 9LQ – slipway on river left at end of Ferry Lane, or anywhere clear of the lock. Park beside the lock. Or on river right (Weybridge side) at slipway TQ 074 657 / KT13 8NG beside Waybridge Dam Car Park, which has a height barrier. Junction of Walton Lane and Thames Street.

Walton Bridge TQ 093 664 / KT12 1BH – slipway river right, upstream of bridge. Cowey Sale car park with height barrier beside Walton Lane.

Walton TQ 098 668 / KT12 2PE – river right in front of The Anglers pub. Limited parking.

Lane off Manor Road. Also on river right at the end of Sunbury Lane TQ 102 674 / KT12 2JQ, limited parking.

Sunbury TQ 104 679 / KT12 2JP – river right, parking area along Waterside Drive. Or launch on river left TQ 115 689 / TW16 5PN from slipway and parking area on river left beside Lower Hampton Road.

West Molesey TQ 142 693 / KT8 9AZ – river right beside car park in Hurst Park. Height barrier at park entrance. End of Sadlers Ride.

Thames Ditton TQ 162 673 / KT7 0QQ - slipway on river right beside Ye Olde Swan Inn. No parking nearby. Or, 400m downstream on river right, slipway TQ 167 671 / KT7 0XB at end of Cholmley Road. Car park with height barrier nearby.

Kingston TQ 176 678 / KT6 4EU – slipway and small car park on river right. A307 Portsmouth Road.

Teddington TQ 171 714 / TW10 7YE – river right from park beside Burnell Ave, 500m before the lock. No slipway, park on road. Or beneath footbridge at end of Ferry Lane TQ 167 714 / TW11 9NN, 150m upstream on river left after passing through the lock; very limited parking. Another option is to continue on the Tideway to Ham Street car park (see Section 14).

Description

The best scenery of this section is directly below Chertsey Bridge; Dumsey Meadow on river left and Chertsey Meads on river right are home to flowers, marsh plants, dandelions and clover, the remnants of more extensive meadows.

📷 *Chertsey Bridge.*

"... the best hay in England; and where, during the large part of the year, there is a right of commonage, of which the neighbouring farmers avail themselves to fatten cows that supply London with pure milk."

Mr and Mrs S.C. Hall,

The Book of the River Thames 1859

The river soon plunges into the wall-to-wall successions of bungalows and mansions, augmented by houseboats, which are characteristic of this section. These are varied and quirky enough to be diverting in their own right, ranging from bland and soulless (did you really fell that willow just to moor your cruiser?) through quaint and ramshackle, passing ostentatious and blingy, to full Bond-villain-hideout ... with a thousand variations in between. The houseboats are often simply mansions on pontoons.

"One of the first desires of the modern occupant of the house-boat is to show how much money they have to squander."

Charles Dickens,

Dictionary of the Thames 1887

Pharaoh's Island, covered by housing and willows, was supposedly gifted to Nelson after the 1798 Battle of the Nile. The river splits three ways, with the middle and right channels leading over weirs and encircling Hamhaugh Island, while the river left channel leads to Shepperton Lock. The lock was created in 1813, seeing tragedy in 1940 when a bomb killed the lock keeper's daughter. There is a café here. Thames River Police are based on Lock Island, which is otherwise a wild haven for water voles. A passenger ferry crosses where the channels re-converge below the lock; this featured in H.G. Wells' 1898 novel,

The War of the Worlds. Watch out for tripods. Eyot House on D'Oyly Carte Island was home to the theatre impresario of the same name, who promoted Gilbert and Sullivan and built the Savoy Theatre. The river splits around Desborough Island with the river right channel entering Desborough Cut, engineered in 1935. Lord Desborough was chairman of the Thames Conservancy, also winning the 1878 Boat Race, swimming the Niagara Rapids, climbing the Matterhorn and rowing the Channel. The Cut bearing his name is a surprising natural interlude, lined by tall trees and high banks.

Walton Bridge is the sixth on this site since 1750. The Thames now passes through a five-kilometre no man's land of waterworks and reservoirs before emerging at Hampton Court Palace and entering Greater London. The main interest comes from the many large islands.

Wheatley's Ait is about 900m long, in several parts divided by weirs. The upstream weir is the rebuilt Tumbling Bay, destroyed by a flying bomb in WWII. Flood Weir is halfway along, with Sunbury Main Weir at the downstream end; this connects to Sunbury Lock Ait which leads another 600m to Sunbury Lock. As this all implies, Sunbury Lock is a monumental piece of engineering; it has been rebuilt numerous times since 1811, with a larger mechanical lock added in 1925. The hand-operated lock still sees use in busy periods. A set of rollers left of the locks make portage easy. Jerome recommended exploring the weir pools: "Sweetly pretty just there before you come

to the gates, and the backwater is charming." (*Three Men in a Boat*, 1889)

Rivermead Island, known as 'Swimming Pool Island' until 1980 when the open air pool closed, is now a park. Its claustrophobic back channel passes Georgian Monksbridge House; Edward VIII reputedly trimmed the topiary teddy bear in the garden for his married mistress living there. Sunbury Court Island which follows directly after is covered by housing. Grand Junction Island was formerly a reservoir intake; reservoirs surround the Thames at this point, hidden from view.

Platt's Eyot is distinctive for the suspension bridge connecting to the river left bank and because it's the Thames' tallest island. Its artificial hill consists of reservoir construction waste. At the east end are some rundown warehouses; this Grade II listed site was Thorneycroft boatyard which constructed 123 fast torpedo boats in WWI, and another 170 in WWII. The first aircraft carrier was built here, a towed platform now in Yeovil's Fleet Air Arm Museum. Platt's Eyot became a conservation area in 1990, to conserve its woodland and breeding song thrushes, and to protect its heritage from the developers.

The Thames bends right at Hampton, passing Benn's Eyot and larger Garrick's Island. The river right shore is Hurst Park, where in 1731 an early cricket match was played. The river left shore leaving Hampton is adorned by an octagonal folly; Garrick's Temple to Shakespeare. David Garrick was an eighteenth-century thespian who commissioned the

📷 *Garrick's Temple.*

temple in 1754 and installed a statue of the playwright inside. Just downstream, the incredible mahogany-framed houseboat with an ornate canopy atop is the Astoria, built in 1911 for Fred Karno (see below) and now a recording studio owned by Dave Gilmour.

Bushy Park on river left is the second largest of London's Royal Parks, created in the sixteenth century to surround Hampton Court Palace. Two large islands lead to Molesey Lock, thronged by multi-storey houseboats. Tagg's Island is guarded at its upstream end by the three willows of tiny Duck Eyot. Tagg was a nineteenth-century owner of the island. His successor Fred Karno opened the Karsino Hotel on the island in 1913, auditioning an unknown Charlie Chaplin. The island became a destination for London's glitterati, known as the

'Thames Riviera'! It was a munitions factory in WWII, and *A Clockwork Orange* was filmed in the hotel before demolition in 1971. Developers moved in and the interior of the island is now a lagoon floating more houseboats. The gap leading to Ash Island is called Hog Hole. Ash Island is greener, taking its name from its trees, with a boatyard alongside Molesey Lock. The lock was rebuilt in 1882 after damage in the Great Flood of 1877. Its eighty-two metre pound is the second longest after Teddington. Rollers are located to the left of the lock.

You're now in front of Hampton Court Palace! Hampton Court Bridge was opened in 1933, designed in red brick and Portland stone by Lutyens to match the palace. Britain's largest palace has witnessed large chunks of England's history; Cardinal Wolsey started building

📷 *Hampton Court Palace from the river.*

it in 1514, Henry VIII confiscated it in 1526 (his son Edward was born, his wife Jane Seymour died, and Katherine Parr was married to Henry here), Mary, Queen of Scots was put on trial here, William and Mary were permanently resident, and Queen Victoria opened it to the public in 1838. Hampton Court deserves several dedicated visits to fully explore it (and to negotiate the 1690 maze which defeated the *Three Men in a Boat*), but from the Thames, you enjoy a good view of Sir Christopher Wren's façade, designed 1656–1704.

The Rivers Mole and Ember join on river right, as the Thames commences a protracted 180 degree bend towards Teddington. Inside the bend is 283 hectare Hampton Court Home Park; look for deer grazing. Wren's red-brick Pavilion of 1700 (a summerhouse for royalty) faces Thames Ditton Island, which has forty-

seven stilted houses crammed onto it. River right of the island, a 1939 suspension bridge leads ashore to the thirteenth-century Olde Swan Inn and eleventh-century St Nicholas Church, with its pointed wooden spire.

Swan Island and Boyle Farm Island follow, both small. The waterworks on river right are Seething Wells; here during the Victorian epidemics, Dr John Snow proved cholera was waterborne. Kingston follows, effectively a single conurbation until Teddington.

Raven's Ait (previously called Raven's Arse!) was likely the site of the 1217 Treaty of Kingston, when the succession of King John's son Henry was agreed (with John in the barons' good books following Magna Carta). The isle has had a chequered recent past; squatters who established a 'community garden' were evicted and an upmarket conference facility has opened.

The bright points in Kingston's uninspiring waterfront are the impressive frontage of St Raphael's Catholic Church (1848) and Kingston Bridge's five arches of gleaming Portland stone (opened 1828, widened 2001). Hampton Court Home Park ends, but the river right shore after Kingston Railway Bridge provides a dose of greenery; Canbury Gardens.

Steven's Eyots are a cluster of long and narrow isles shrouded in willows. From 1872 they were a nude bathing area for men, with screens erected for modesty. Since 1953, they have been home to the quirky Small Boat Club. Trowlock Island nestles into the river left bank and could easily be missed; however the first building is home to Royal Canoe Club, established in 1866 by John MacGregor and based here since 1897. The rest of the island includes some rare century-old weekend chalets.

Traffic lights welcome you as you approach Teddington Lock. Those who have paddled from Cricklade may struggle to process the urban-hemmed expanse that the Thames has become in its final leg to the Tideway.

Variations

Some exploring is possible around **Hamhaugh Island** and up the Wey Navigation. **Desborough Island**, an uninhabited 45 hectare nature reserve shrouded by trees, offers a 3.5 kilometre circuit. The 'outside' bank passes Shepperton's Church Square, with St Nicholas' Church built in 1614 on piles in the river mud, opposite the King's Head where Charles II and Nell Gwyn met. The white building fronted by perfect lawns and willows is eighteenth-century Shepperton Manor.

 Steven's Eyots.

The Tideway

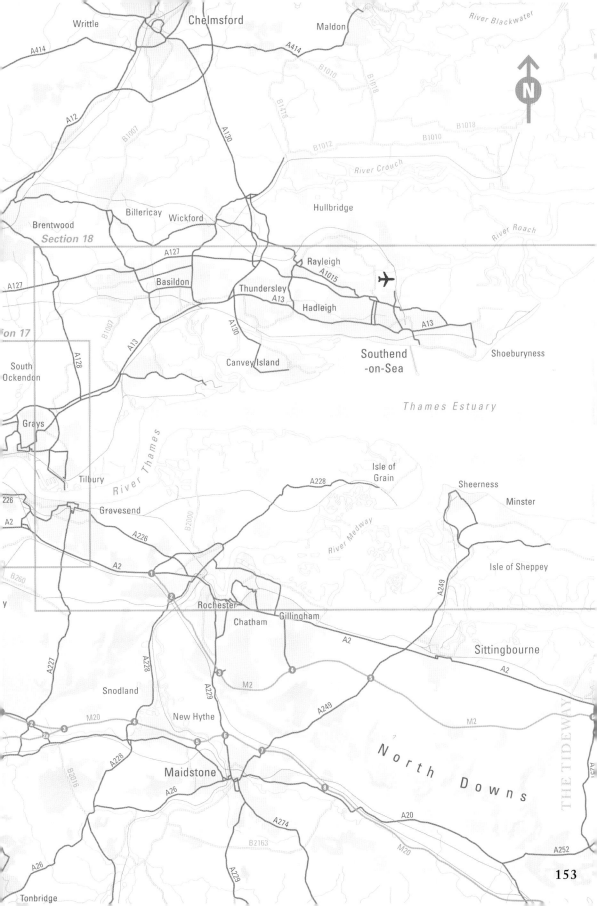

Writtle

Chelmsford

Maldon

River Blackwater

A414

A414

B1010

B1018

B1018

A12

B1007

A130

B1418

B1012

B1010

River Crouch

N

Billericay

Wickford

Hullbridge

River Roach

Brentwood

Section 18

A127

Rayleigh

A127

Basildon

Thundersley

A1015

South Ockendon

B1007

A13

A13

Hadleigh

A13

Shoeburyness

on 17

A128

Canvey Island

Southend -on-Sea

A130

Grays

River Thames

Thames Estuary

226

Tilbury

Isle of Grain

Sheerness

A228

Minster

A2

Gravesend

B2000

River Medway

B260

A226

A2

Isle of Sheppey

1

A227

A228

2

Rochester

Gillingham

A2

Sittingbourne

Chatham

A2

Snodland

A229

M2

3

4

5

A249

M2

THE TIDEWAY

M20

New Hythe

M2

A249

2

3

4

6

7

North Downs

A251

22

5

8

A228

B2016

Maidstone

A26

A20

A274

M20

A252

153

B2163

A229

Tonbridge

A26

Teddington to Putney Bridge

Distance 17.9km

Start △ Teddington TQ 171 714 / TW10 7YE

Finish ○ Putney Bridge TQ 238 758 / SW15 1LB

Introduction

The Thames above Putney might be the quietest place and greenest place in London! Landscaped gardens, mansions and intriguing islands maintain interest throughout.

Launch points

Teddington TQ 171 714 / TW10 7YE – river right from park beside Burnell Ave, 500m before the lock. No slipway, park on road. Or beneath footbridge at end of Ferry Lane TQ 167 714 / TW11 9NN, 150m upstream on river left after passing through the lock; very limited parking.

Twickenham Drawdock TQ 164 732 / TW1 3NX – slipway at junction of Church Lane and Riverside into channel river left of Eel Pie Island. Limited parking close by.

Twickenham, White Swan Drawdock TQ 168 733 / TW1 3DL – river left slipway opposite White Swan pub. Limited parking close by.

Richmond, Ham Street car park TQ 170 732 / TW1 3DJ – slipways on river right in large car park with height barrier, end of Ham Street. Park on road outside barrier. Car park subject to flooding at spring tides.

Petersham, River Lane Drawdock TQ 178 735 / TW10 7AQ – slipway river right at end of River Lane, park on road.

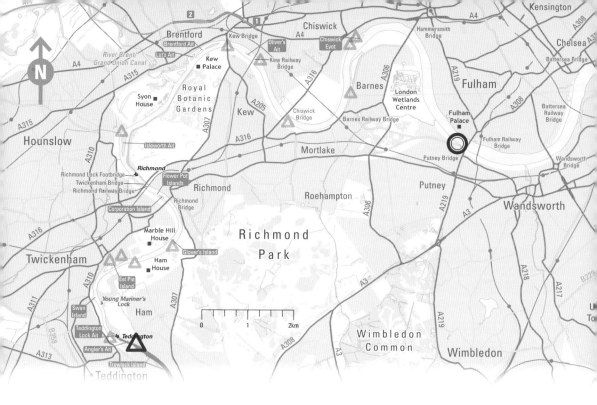

Isleworth Drawdock TQ 167 760 / TW7 6BE – slipway on Church Street into river left channel behind Isleworth Ait. Plenty of parking.

Kew Bridge Drawdock TQ 190 779 / W4 3NG – slipway on river left downstream of bridge, park on Strand-on-the-Green.

Grove Park Drawdock TQ 197 774 / W4 3QD – slipway on river left, junction of Thames Road and Grove Park Road. Parking all round.

Mortlake, Ship Lane Drawdock TQ 204 761 / SW14 7QW – slipway on river right opposite Ship Inn, junction of Thames Bank and Ship Lane. Parking all round.

Barnes, Small Profits Drawdock TQ 216 767 / SW13 9QB – slipway on river right alongside B350. Park in lay-by.

Chiswick Church Drawdock TQ 216 777 / W4 9BZ – slipway on river left beside church, junction of Church Street and Chiswick Mall. Limited parking nearby.

Chiswick Drawdock TQ 217 779 / W4 2PW – slipway on Chiswick Mall into channel river left of Chiswick Eyot. Limited parking nearby, channel dries at low tide.

Putney Bridge TQ 238 758 / SW15 1LB – slipway 200m upstream of bridge on river right, on Embankment opposite Chas Newens Marine. Limited parking.

Description

Teddington Lock's three chambers range from the 198m Barge Lock (built in 1904) to the 15m Skiff Lock. For paddlers, rollers in the centre make portage easy.

River right below the lock, trees filled with parakeets (really!) line the shore for the first two kilometres. This is Ham Lands, open grasslands reclaimed from refilled gravel pits. About 250m along this shore is an obelisk marking the start of the Port of London's jurisdiction. A little further, Young Mariners Lock is the entrance to a tidal lake and outdoor adventure centre.

Eel Pie Island (the name refers to a dish served at the island's inn in the eighteenth century) is surrounded by willows, with nature reserves at both ends. The upstream reserve ('The Wilderness') features an artificial sand cliff for martins and bats. Prehistoric artefacts have been unearthed on the island, but its iconic fame derives from recent times. From the 1950s until its dilapidated remains burned down in 1971, Eel Pie Hotel was a music venue-turned-hippy commune where newcomers such as the Rolling Stones, Fairport Convention, Rod Stewart, David Bowie, Eric Clapton, Jimmy Page, Pink Floyd, Deep Purple and The Who performed.

The river left channel behind Eel Pie passes eighteenth-century St Mary's Church, a red-brick classical design where Alexander Pope is buried. Adjacent, but mostly hidden from view is York House, a 1663 Palladian mansion. Every September since 1988, Ham Street car park on river right has seen the finish of the Great River Race, where all manner of small craft race from Greenwich.

The Thames flows along Horse Reach between the landscaped grounds of two mansions, the view ahead adorned by the Star and Garter on Richmond Hill, built between 1921

Richmond Hill.

and 1924 as a home for disabled servicemen, and now refurbished as luxury apartments. Ham House (river right) was built in 1610 and is virtually unaltered. Marble Hill House (river left) is a showpiece of Palladian classicism, built in 1723 for George II's mistress Henrietta Howard. Beneath Richmond Hill, Petersham Meadows is the last place where cows graze in London. Glover's Island is now wooded but was boosted in the nineteenth century by tube excavation rubble; Glover was an entrepreneurial owner who attempted to blackmail the council into buying it by threatening to host Pears Soap advertising hoardings! This lead to Richmond Hill's view being protected by law (1902), a legal first. What a view! Turner painted it, Wordsworth eulogised it and Dickens wrote: "Nothing in the neighbourhood of London is better known or more delightful than the view from Richmond Hill."

Richmond Bridge is the oldest in Greater London, its five arches designed by James Paine in 1777. Corporation Island gained its name in 1890 when Richmond became a borough; now it's a quiet spot for birdlife. The weeny Flower Pot Islands just downstream

157

📷 *Near Mortlake.*

are remnants of a single island. Beside them on river right is Asgill House, built in 1758 for Lord Mayor Sir Charles Asgill.

Richmond Railway Bridge sits alongside Twickenham Road Bridge, just above Richmond half-tide Lock. A mechanical weir suspended between two five-arched footbridges, this beauty of Victorian engineering has rendered good service since 1894.

For four kilometres to Kew Bridge, the river right shore follows Kew's parkland and gardens; the Old Deer Park, then the Royal Botanical Gardens (created in 1841 and housing 178,000 plants, 1/8th of known species!) and finally Kew Palace itself, built in 1631 and the smallest Royal Palace. The river left bank leads past Syon House, the Duke of Northumberland's home, where Lady Jane Grey became queen for nine days and dogs savaged Henry VIII's body during its funerary procession to Windsor; only the classical boathouse/pavilion is seen as the banks are surprisingly overgrown. After Syon Reach, the River Brent and Grand Union Canal join above Brentford, where the most recognisable landmark is the ornate brickwork of Kew Bridge Steam Museum Tower.

For paddlers, the main interest between Richmond Lock and Kew Bridge is the islands:

- Isleworth Ait (pronounced eye-zul-worth) is 500m long, opposite the seventeenth-century London Apprentice pub. Landing on this London Wildlife Trust reserve is forbidden without permission; fifty-seven species of bird are found among the cypress

📷 *Brentford Ait.*

and poplars (and also a redwood tree, presumably escaped from Kew). However, snails are the exciting bit. The two-lipped door snail is extremely rare, and when the German hairy snail was found here in 1983, it had been presumed extinct in Britain.

- The Brentford Islands are two kilometres downstream. The river scenes in *The African Queen* (1951) were filmed here, which sounds absurd until you experience this London wilderness! Lot's Ait has a mix of woodland and derelict workshops where activities including traditional boatbuilding occasionally take place; a friend built a kayak here! Brentford Ait is 600m long, with a gap in the middle (Hog's Hole) covering at high tide. It is densely draped in willows, plane trees, alders and poplars with a large heronry in the treetops. Brentford Ait owes its lush greenery to Kew Palace residents' desire to obscure Brentford; the trees were planted as a screen.

Kew Bridge, built in 1903, is properly called Edward VII Bridge. To its right is the 1714 spire of St Anne's Church, where Gainsborough is buried. Henceforth trees still border the river, but the city intrudes more.

The colourful eighteenth-century houses of Strand-on-the-Green on river left (guarded by flood barriers) lead to Oliver's Ait, a London Natural History Society reserve covered with willows and poplars where cormorants and woodpeckers nest. Oliver Cromwell supposedly sought refuge here, arriving via a tunnel from the Bull's Head pub, downstream on river left. On the same bank, the City Barge pub (1497) hails back to the late eighteenth century when a barge at Oliver's Ait collected tolls; traces of the tollhouse survive on the island.

Kew Railway Bridge and Chiswick Bridge are passed. Some 113m past the latter on river right, a stone marked UBR denotes the Boat Race course's end. The Thames bends left past Duke's Meadows on river left and Mortlake on river right; Mortlake Reach and Corney Reach past Barnes Bridge (an 1895 railway bridge) are an attractive enclave of quiet greenery.

On river left, the start of Georgian Chiswick Mall is marked by St Nicholas's Church, where Hogarth and J.M. Whistler are buried. Number 26 was Kelmscott House, London home (and in 1894, place of death) of William Morris. He named the house after his manor on the Upper Thames (see Section 2), which he rowed upstream to in 1880 and 1881.

Chiswick Reach leads past Chiswick Eyot, known as "the first island in the Thames" by boatmen; of course, it's the last. Well into the twentieth century, willows were harvested here and the back channel used for fish trapping. Basket makers still cut osier rods here. A great lunch spot, but note that the back channel dries.

Hammersmith Bridge is the finest on this section, an ornate green-gold suspension bridge, designed by Sir Joseph Bazalgette and opened in 1887. With 3.6m clearance, it is the lowest in London. Irish Republicans tried to blow it up *three* times during the twentieth century; one

 Oliver's Ait.

📷 *Hammersmith Bridge.*

attempt was foiled when a hero-citizen lobbed the suitcase-bomb into the Thames, producing a twenty-metre plume of water.

For the three kilometres of Barn Elms Reach to Putney Bridge, old quays and docks line the shores. The Harrods Furniture Depository (now apartments) is a quirky landmark on river right, which is followed (unseen except for the increase in wildfowl) by the London Wetland Centre, established on reclaimed reservoirs. On river left, little stands out (unless Craven Cottage, stadium of Fulham FC excites you) but you pass Tudor red-brick Fulham Palace, until the 1970s the home of the Bishops of London.

A succession of rowing clubs line the river right bank approaching Putney Bridge; the final slipway is public.

The Arcadian Thames

Hampton to Kew has been labelled the 'Arcadian Thames'. During the seventeenth and eighteenth centuries, palaces and mansions developed through royal and noble patronage, at a safe distance from London's stench and diseases. What is remarkable was their manufactured landscape; the buildings were surrounded by parks and gardens attempting to recreate 'Arcadia', an idealistic vision of pastoral perfection. Naturally this vision did not tolerate the presence of commoners (beyond the occasional decorative shepherd), but the highlights of this movement are now mostly open to the public; Hampton Court, Syon House, Ham House, Marble Hill, Strawberry Hill and Kew Palace.

Big Ben.

© Lambeth Bridge.

Putney Bridge to Shadwell Basin

Distance	15.3km
Start	△ Putney Bridge TQ 238 758 / SW15 1LB
Finish	○ Shadwell Basin TQ 354 805 / E1W 3TF

Introduction

Paddling through London's heart is a serious undertaking requiring careful planning. The experience of viewing our capital (and history) from this breathtaking perspective, effectively on fast-forward, is unforgettable.

Launch points

Putney Bridge TQ 238 758 / SW15 1LB – slipway 200m upstream of bridge on river right, on Embankment opposite Chas Newens Marine. Limited parking.

Fulham, Broomhouse Drawdock TQ 253 755 / SW6 3EJ – inlet on river left at end of Broomhouse Lane, parking on road nearby.

Battersea Church Drawdock TQ 268 768 / SW11 3ND – slipway on river right beside church, Battersea Church Road. Limited parking nearby.

Shadwell Basin TQ 354 805 / E1W 3TF – small beach on river left with steps to Thames Path. No parking close by, and likely none at all outside weekends. No beach at high tide.

Description

Putney Bridge was another of Joseph Bazalgette's designs (1886), replacing a wooden toll bridge from which in 1795 Mary Wollstonecraft attempted suicide. There are churches at both ends; All Saints on river left in Fulham and St Mary's on river right in Putney, whose 1440 spire caused a grisly death in the 1976 movie *The Omen*. Since 1845, the bridge has also seen the start of the Boat Race. The Head of the River Race finishes here, the biggest rowing event in the world (over 400 crews).

Below Fulham Railway Bridge is the Wandsworth Reach; enjoy the plane trees lining Wandsworth Park and the muddy confluence of the River Wandle, as after Wandsworth Bridge (1940, judged the dullest on the river), the speed limit and traffic increase and there is less time for nature-watching.

Battersea Reach leads below Battersea Railway Bridge, with Chelsea Harbour on river left. On river right, St Mary's Church (1777) might be the author's favourite Tideway sight. London's only riverside church sits atop a beach, backdropped by high-rise glass. William Blake was married here (1782) and Benedict Arnold (for Americans, a byword for treachery) lies in the crypt. Chelsea Creek on river left led to Lots Road Power Station, decommissioned in 2002 and since converted into flats.

Gold-green Battersea Bridge (1890) is another monument to Bazalgette's engineering, as are the embankments which follow. While London's iconic embankments are undeniably appealing with their promenades, statues, cast iron lamps and benches, they aren't merely decorative; Bazalgette incorporated

📷 St Mary's Church, Battersea.

sewage removal tunnels, while also narrowing the river and covering the foreshore to accelerate the flow.

The 'wavy' glass apartments on river right are the Albion Riverside Building, designed by Sir Norman Foster. Chelsea Old Church on river left is not much older, having been reconstructed after destruction by a Blitz bomb.

Sir John Betjeman described Albert Bridge: "Shining with electric lights, grey and airy against the London sky, it is one of the beauties of the London River." The author's earliest memory of London is of the 4000+ bulbs illuminating Rowland Ordish's 1873 cantilever and suspension design. Day or night, Albert Bridge is really something.

Chelsea Reach threads between Wren's 1682 Chelsea Royal Hospital on river left, and Battersea Park on river right. The park has hosted both a duel involving a Prime Minister (the Duke of Wellington, 1829) and the 1951 Festival of Britain. Now it is fronted by the thirty metre-high Peace Pagoda, opened by Japanese Buddhist monks on the 40th anniversary of the Hiroshima bombing. Buddha sits above the river, contemplating human folly.

Chelsea Bridge (a 1937 suspension bridge) and Grosvenor Bridge (an 1859 rail bridge, rebuilt 1967) lead to Nine Elms Reach, where London's most monolithic building towers on river right. Battersea Power Station, Europe's biggest brick building, was built 1929–39 to Charles Gilbert Scott's Art Deco design. Since it closed in 1983, debate has raged; what to do with it? At the time of writing, the four 103m chimneys are being reconstructed and the power station redeveloped for housing and offices, including the addition of a taxi pier.

[📷] *MI6 Building.*

The River Tyburn, which gave its name to London's gallows, trickles in on river left above Vauxhall Bridge (1906). Five steel arches rest on granite piers, adorned with figures representing science and art; look for the woman holding a model of St Paul's. The bridge dates from 1906 but Bronze Age oak posts have been uncovered here, traces of London's oldest bridge.

The Art Deco-styled MI6 Building on river right was opened in 1995. Not the most discreet spy HQ, it has attracted several terrorist attacks. Across the river, several significant buildings lead to Lambeth Bridge. The classical pillars of the 1897 Tate Britain Gallery are followed by Millbank Tower (a 118m early tower block, 1963), Thames House (MI5 HQ) and Imperial Chemical House (Art Deco, the 'ICI' building). Lambeth Bridge (1932) is red and gold, the pillars at end eccentrically topped with pineapples.

Lambeth Reach is hard to mistake! On river right is the red-brick Tudor gatehouse of Lambeth Palace. This has been the Archbishop of Canterbury's residence since the twelfth century. Opposite begins the 287m river frontage of the Palace of Westminster; the Houses of Parliament and the 98m high Elizabeth Tower more commonly known as Big Ben. **Don't** cross the yellow markers, this is the only restricted area on the river! The palace was opened in 1859, the design and decor by Charles Barry and his assistant Pugin responsible for starting the Gothic revival. It is currently undergoing restoration; estimates of the final cost run into billions.

Westminster Bridge (1862) is the start of what the Port of London Authority call 'The Heart of London', as if you weren't already there! However, this fairly refers to the intensive traffic and powerful tidal conditions (and eleven bridges) encountered in the four kilometres to Tower Bridge. In particular, be wary of piers where cruisers speedily arrive and leave; only those encountered on river right are mentioned below.

Below Westminster Bridge, the steps on river right leading to County Hall will be very familiar to Devizes to Westminster veterans. Behind, the 135m London Eye is fronted by Waterloo Pier. It is not possible to paddle behind this, approach and pass with extreme care.

Tattershall Castle, 1934 Humber paddle steamer and now a restaurant, is moored on river left above Hungerford Bridge. This grimy 1860's rail bridge is adorned either side by the attractive suspension struts of the Golden Jubilee Bridges, footbridges added in 2003. Charing Cross Station is on river left; the arched 1980's office block above recalls the former station roof.

Eighteen-metre Cleopatra's Needle has sat atop the river left embankment since 1878 (dating from 1500 BC, nothing to do with Cleopatra). Across King's Reach it faces the Brutalist 1950s concrete of the Southbank Centre,

Approaching Blackfriars Bridge.

a remnant of the 1951 Festival of Britain and fronted on the river by the Royal Festival Hall and Queen Elizabeth Hall, with the National Theatre continuing the 'multi-storey car park' style below Waterloo Bridge.

Giles Gilbert Scott's Waterloo Bridge was opened on the anniversary of the battle in 1945; it is also known as 'The Ladies Bridge' as women carried out the construction work during WWII. HQS *Wellington*, a gleaming white restored WWII convoy ship, is moored on river left below. The view ahead at this point is jaw dropping, with St Paul's Cathedral vying for attention among a forest of variously-shaped skyscrapers.

The Thames from St Paul's Cathedral.

📷 *Tower Bridge sunset.*

The river narrows at Blackfriars Bridge (1869, look for swans and herons carved in the Portland Stone), causing waves. Blackfriars Railway Bridge is directly after and then you are sandwiched between 111m high St Paul's Cathedral (Wren, 1708) on river left, and the Tate Modern with its central brick tower (formerly Bankside Power Station) on river right. They are joined by the slender Millennium Bridge, opened 2000 and then altered and reopened 2002 because Londoners found it 'wobbly'. Just after, the replica of Shakespeare's Globe Theatre (opened 1997) on river right is fronted by Bankside Pier, which you have the option to pass inside or (preferably) outside.

Yellow and green Southwark Bridge (1921), Cannon Street Railway Bridge (1866) and London Bridge pass in quick succession (1973). Waves are common along this reach, with the foundations of London Bridge's predecessors disrupting the water.

If you aren't already catatonic from scenic overload, the Upper Pool leading to Tower Bridge will make you so. Above on river right, the Shard reaches its 310m apex. Britain's tallest building still fails to distract from HMS *Belfast*, Tower Bridge itself and on river left, the Tower of London.

📷 *HMS Belfast.*

An immediate hazard is London Bridge City Pier; pass behind if possible. If you then continue behind HMS *Belfast* (conditions permitting), you can rest and absorb your surroundings. This 11,000 ton battle-cruiser was launched in 1938, helped sink the Scharnhorst and fired ashore on D-Day. Downstream, London's mayor watches from the glass dome of Norman Foster's 2002 City Hall.

On river left, the 1078 White Tower rears over the walls of the Tower of London, with Traitor's Gate (now sealed) at water level. From 1934 to 1971 the foreshore served as an artificial beach, deckchairs and all, with 1500 tons of sand used annually. This in an era when the Thames was not at its cleanest ...

Horace Jones' gothic Tower Bridge opened in 1894 (to considerable revulsion at the time). The 1,000 ton lifting bridges give forty-three metres of clearance for passing shipping. The elevated walkways above were closed in 1910 as they were frequented by thieves and prostitutes. Given twenty-four hours' notice, London VTS can lift the bridges for you, although we don't recommend asking.

The river widens below Tower Bridge, both banks lined by former warehouses, now eye-wateringly expensive flats. You can relax somewhat (having survived the previous melee) but keep an eye out for fast traffic.

Bermondsey on river right is where J.M.W. Turner painted *The Fighting Temeraire* in 1838. According to Dickens the River Neckinger was the worst place to live in London;

"the Venice of Drains" saw half of cholera deaths. Cherry Garden Pier marks the start of the Lower Pool, with the pierced spire of St Mary's Church (1715, burial place of the *Mayflower's* captain) indicating that you've reached Rotherhithe.

The river left shore below Tower Bridge is Wapping. St Katharine Docks were designed by Telford and opened in 1828, after 11,300 people were evicted without compensation. It's now a marina. The Town of Ramsgate pub is followed by the HQ of Thames River Police, and then the splendid Prospect of Whitby, London's oldest riverside pub (1560). Somewhere along Wapping's shore is the site of Execution Dock. For 400 years until 1830, pirates were hanged by a short rope and left hanging for three tides. The site is disputed, contenders including both above-named pubs.

If you are landing at Shadwell Basin, cross the river with care.

The Marchioness disaster

During the night of 20th August 1989, the *Marchioness* was rammed by the dredger *Bowbelle* near Cannon Street Railway Bridge. Fifty-one of the party-goers onboard were killed. The *Bowbelle's* skipper was later exonerated of wrongdoing, despite having drunk five pints of lager that evening. This tragedy increased awareness of the dangers of the London Thames and directly led to the establishing of lifeboat stations in London.

Old Royal Naval College.

Approaching the Thames Barrier.

Shadwell Basin to Woolwich

Distance   12.5km

Start   △ Shadwell Basin TQ 354 805 / E1W 3TF

Finish   ◯ Woolwich TQ 434 793 / SE18 6DL

Introduction

"It takes on a new and more sombre form of glory, assumes a mightier interest, and is infinitely more majestic in the lifting of its waters ... the water surges and heaves in broad masses."

Anon, *The Royal River* 1885

The now quieter river is hemmed in by walls and wharves, but with a spectacular backdrop. Passing through the Thames Flood Barrier is an unforgettable experience.

Launch points

Shadwell Basin TQ 354 805 / E1W 3TF – small beach on river left with steps to Thames Path. No parking close by, and likely none at all outside weekends. No beach at high tide, potentially an awkward launch.

Isle of Dogs, Millwall Slipway TQ 372 791 / E14 3QS – large slipway on river left opposite Docklands Sailing Centre on Westferry Road. No parking close by.

Isle of Dogs, Newcastle Drawdock TQ 386 785 / E14 3EA – large slipway on river left at junction of Saunders Ness Road and Glenaffric Avenue, limited parking nearby.

Greenwich, Warspite Road TQ 420 793 / SE18 5NX – slipway on river right directly downstream of Thames Barrier, accessed via stairs at end of Warspite Road. No parking close by.

Woolwich TQ 434 793 / SE18 6DL – Bell Water Gate; slipway on river right, on lane off A206, east of Waterfront Leisure Centre. Car park at end of lane.

North Woolwich TQ 438 799 / E16 2NW – Bargehouse Causeway; slipway on river left, at end of Barge House Road. Limited parking on road in urban surrounds.

Description

Cherry Garden Pier (the bend before Shadwell Basin) to Island Jetty (just before the Barrier) is the Lower Rowing Code Area; where rowers 'work the slacks', on the inside of bends rather than the starboard shore. Where possible, give them space to pass inside. There are a number of piers, where cruisers arrive and leave with haste; where possible, pass these on the inside.

You are paddling through Docklands' ghost. The thousands of ships which once obscured the river below Tower Bridge are long gone, although the warehouses still line both shores, gentrified into 'yuppie' apartments. Joseph Conrad's nineteenth-century description still has validity: "It recalls a jungle by the confused, varied and impenetrable aspect of the buildings that line the shore, not according to a planned purpose, but as sprung up by accident."

The key difference is the skyscrapers of Canary Wharf, looming over the Isle of Dogs and dominating the view from Shadwell Basin. The tallest, One Canada Square, reaches 235m. Opened in 1991, Canary Wharf was seen by many as the death of working class docker culture and the imposition of Thatcherite greed and upward mobility.

📷 *Rotherhithe.*

River left is Limehouse Marina, where the Regent's Canal joins. The area around this 1820 Dock was notorious for Chinese brothels and opium dens frequented by sailors. The sixteenth-century Grapes pub (formerly the Bunch of Grapes) was described by Dickens in *Our Mutual Friend*: "A tavern of dropsical appearance ... the whole house impended over the water but seemed to have got into the condition of a faint-hearted diver, who has paused so long on the brink that he will never go in at all." The description still holds good.

Opposite on river right, the Rotherhithe Peninsula's tip is known as Cuckold's Point; King John misbehaved here. Keep inshore as two cruiser piers face each other; Nelson Dock Pier on the river right Rotherhithe shore, and Canary Wharf Pier on the Isle of Dogs.

You'll paddle around the Isle of Dogs for the following six kilometres. It has only been an 'island' since the 1805 opening of West India Dock's east entrance, cutting through the Millwall peninsula. It is so-named as Henry VIII had kennels here, or possibly it was originally the Isle of Ducks! Some of the huge docks built to accommodate larger ships have been filled in; others survive providing important birdlife habitats.

Greenland Pier on river right is followed by Greenland Dock's entrance; a reference to the eighteenth-century whaling industry. Just after, a spherical mesh of wire on a platform is the first of various large art installations.

Across the river is Millwall and West India Docks' entrance. Masthouse Terrace Pier and Burrell's Wharf are where in 1858 Brunel's

206m SS *Great Eastern*, then the largest ship ever built, was slowly and arduously launched sideways. Traces of the launch ramp survive behind the waterfront.

Deptford, on river right, is the site of Henry VIII's dockyard where in 1581, Elizabeth I knighted Drake after sailing around the world on the *Golden Hind*. Today it's mostly uninspiring industry. The Ravensbourne River joins via muddy Deptford Creek, and Greenwich is reached:

"Like a jewel of unexampled lustre in that drab scenario between Surrey Commercial Docks and Blackwall Reach."

H.J. Massingham, *London Scene* 1934

Greenwich is a World Heritage Site worthy of a visit in its own right, but enough can be seen from the water to give the flavour of the place.

Steps and beaches near the *Cutty Sark* can be used if you fancy a proper explore.

The *Cutty Sark* sits above the water on a see-through platform, just before Greenwich Pier. Named for the scanty chemise worn by its figurehead, it was the last clipper ship to transport tea from India and China. It has suffered various misfortunes since leaving the water in 1954 (not least two fires) but has been impressively restored.

Greenwich's Palace of Placentia was where Henry VIII and his daughter Elizabeth were born. In the seventeenth century William II's wife Mary commissioned Wren to design the current Baroque complex; it was used charitably as a home for disabled sailors. From 1873 it became the Royal Naval College and more recently, some parts have become the

📷 *Old Royal Naval College.*

University of Greenwich. The Old Royal Naval College is open to the public, with free entry. Behind is the National Maritime Museum, overlooked by Charles II's Greenwich Park. Atop the hill, the Royal Observatory (created for Royal Astronomer Flamsteed) famously sits on the Greenwich Meridian, although this imaginary line was only agreed (at a Washington DC conference) in 1884.

If you wish to delay paddling across the Meridian, the Trafalgar (a favourite of Dickens) and Yacht pubs overlook the river.

Greenwich Power Station is a quite a shock; a towering four-chimneyed black monolith encroaching into the river. The river right bank is now industry and wharves (some working, some abandoned) as the river leads north along Blackwall Reach. At the

Greenwich Peninsula's end is the O2 Arena, formerly known as the Millennium Dome. Measuring 320m in diameter with twelve 100m masts, it isn't pretty but nor is it boring. Note the waterfront, where the Environment Agency resisted the temptation to build more concrete walls and instead created stepped banks where reeds now grow thickly; a template for future restorations.

📷 *O2 Arena.*

📷 *Thames Barrier.*

A permanently-moored vertical slice of former sand dredger *Arco Trent* (15% of it, to be precise) will make you do a double-take. This is *A Slice of Reality*, an art installation by Richard Wilson.

Rounding Blackwall Point, you enter the Thames Barrier Control Zone and are expected to notify London VTS that you're approaching the Barrier.

On river left, the red-brick lighthouse just before the River Lea joins is Trinity Buoy Wharf, now disused but built 1864–6 by James Douglass; the only lighthouse on the Thames. Trinity Jubilee Pier is just below.

The Thames Flood Barrier

During the 1953 North Sea storm, a 2.4m tide surge killed 307 people around the estuary. London's vulnerability was recognised and a barrier recommended; however a gate wide enough to accommodate Dockland shipping was impractical. Only in 1974 after the ascension of Tilbury Docks did work begin. Opened in 1984, the 523m wide edifice has ten gates. The six central gates comprise two thirty metre spans and four 61.5m wide 3,700 tonne steel gates which hydraulically rotate up from the river bed. The Barrier closed twice a year on average to 1990, and about five times a year since. By February 2016, it had shut 176 times. It's estimated that it can handle rising sea levels until 2060–70.

North Greenwich Pier on river right is the last terminal (no more avoiding fast cruisers!), accompanied by a jumble of wiring on a platform; the Quantum Cloud art installation. Directly following, a white pylon rears 60m straight from the river, surrounded by buffers. This supports the Emirates Air Line, a 1,100m long cable car across the river. Costing £60 million, and of questionable value to London's transport infrastructure, this has proved controversial.

The Barrier hoves into view along Woolwich Reach; your focus will be on lining up for the correct gate (see Paddling the Tideway). On river left is Silvertown, site of Royal Victoria Docks and industry undergoing redevelopment. The movies *Full Metal Jacket* and *Brazil* were filmed here, Silvertown standing in for Saigon and a futuristic dystopia, respectively.

📷 *Woolwich.*

Large jetties and wharves line the Woolwich shore on river right approaching the Barrier; be careful. Just before passing through, turn around and appreciate the wide vista of London's skyscrapers; it's quite something.

The view ahead to Woolwich is less edifying; paddle past these tower blocks – remain alert crossing the ferry route! – and look for your landing.

📷 *Woolwich.*

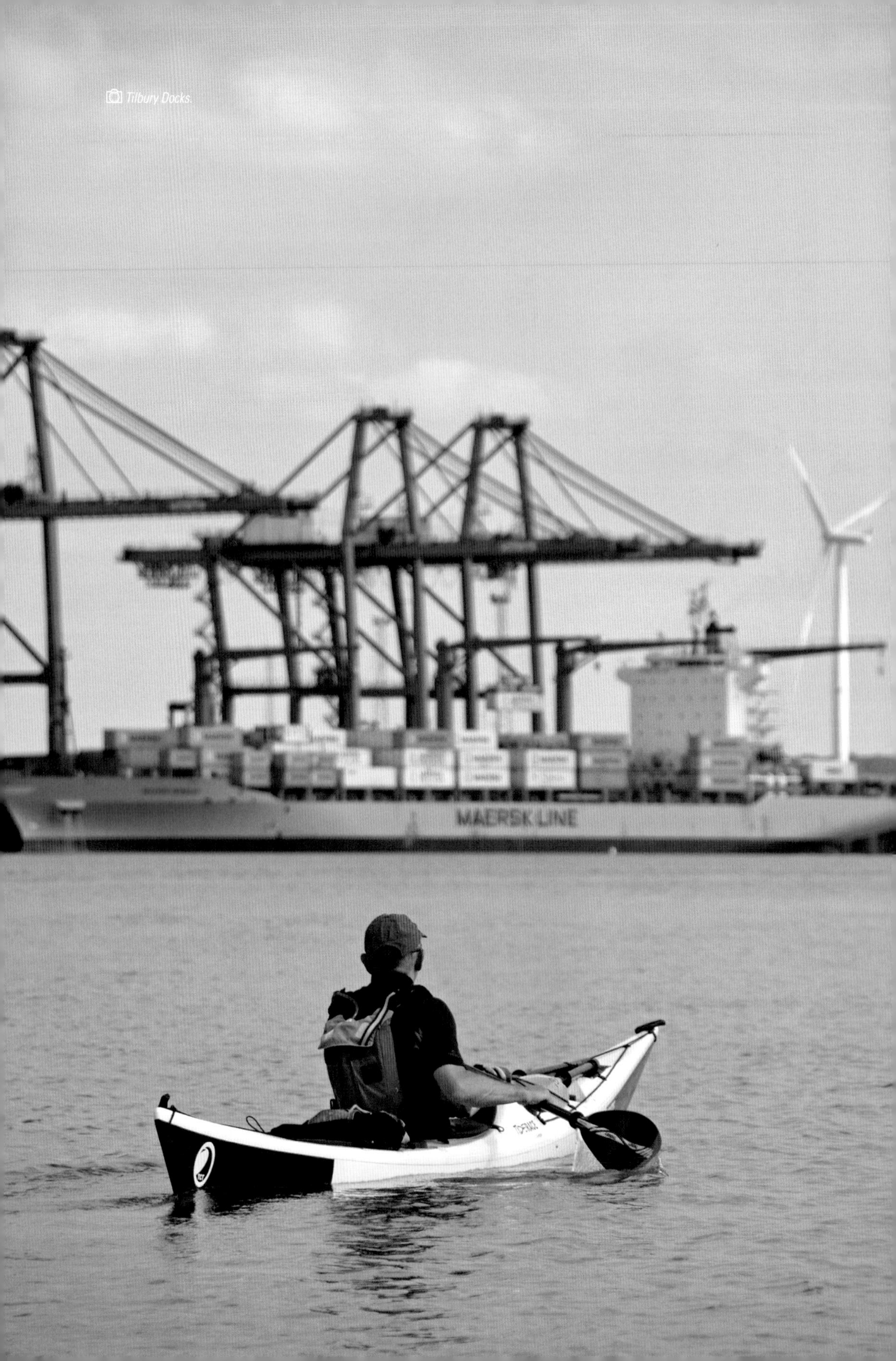

Tilbury Docks.

Below Crayford Ness.

Woolwich to Gravesend

Distance	27.2km
Start	△ Woolwich TQ 434 793 / SE18 6DL
Finish	○ Gravesend TQ 652 744 / DA12 2BS

Introduction

Welcome to the Thames Gateway! This forgotten and neglected corner of south-east England is characterised by industrial wasteland, marsh and open horizons. It is slated for redevelopment; massive amounts of new housing. Explore this vast landscape while you can, because – you'll only believe this by experiencing it for yourself – it's simply beautiful.

Launch points

Woolwich TQ 434 793 / SE18 6DL – Bell Water Gate; slipway on river right, on lane off A206, east of Waterfront Leisure Centre. Car park at end of lane.

North Woolwich TQ 438 799 / E16 2NW – Bargehouse Causeway; slipway on river left at end of Barge House Road. Limited parking on road in urban surrounds.

Erith Causeway TQ 515 781 / DA8 1SB – slipway on river right. Beside Erith High Street, parking across the street.

Greenhithe Causeway TQ 588 752 / DA9 9NS – slipway on river right. Behind Pier Hotel on High Street, ask hotel for permission to park.

Gravesend TQ 652 744 / DA12 2BS – wooden slipway on river right leading past Rowing Club to small parking area.

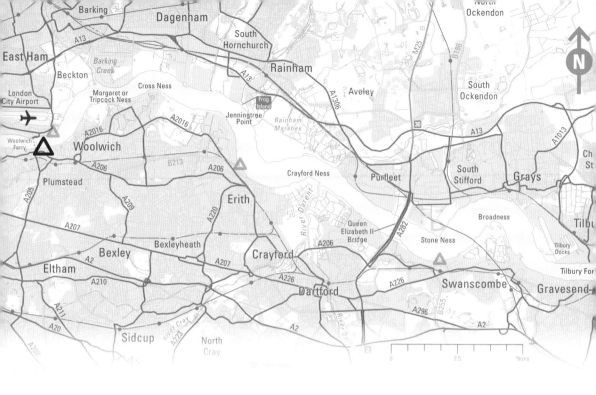

Description

Safety is paramount on this trip and it needs to be carefully planned. The river is wider and more exposed than previously, often resembling a lake. The mud banks expand as the tide falls; sometimes they are firm enough to walk on, usually they aren't. Of greatest concern is the traffic; 14,000 ships a year pass through, carrying c.50 million tons. These ships are exponentially larger than anything encountered on the Thames so far, and you should not be anywhere near. You will need to adhere to the rules of the road, which means remaining on the starboard side (right-hand bank, looking in your direction of travel), at all times keeping clear of the buoyed channel.

The first few kilometres give the flavour of this section; cruising with the tide, far enough offshore to keep clear of the numerous jetties, aiming for a distant headland ('Ness') marking

a bend in the river, with industrialised shores some distance away. The first headland is Tripcock Ness, on river right. It is marked by a red tower/light and although there is extensive industrial land behind, the face presented to the river is verdant and lush; this proves to be the case for much of the journey.

The surrounding mudflats are anything but barren. In winter, huge populations of waders and other birds congregate along the shore; lapwing, heron, shelduck, little grebe, snipe, dunlin, black-tailed godwit, bar-tailed godwit, teal, redshank, water pipit and oystercatcher. They share the mud with populations of grey and common seals.

Barking Creek joins on river left beneath a huge barrier, raised like a bridge. This was opened in 1982, part of the Thames Barrier flood defence system.

Tripcock Ness.

Rounding Cross Ness, the river left bank is Dagenham, site of the Ford plant since 1931. This is followed by the jetties of Frog Island, a waste management facility, and then the Tilda Factory (yes, where rice comes from), with a cluster of former D-Day barges abandoned in the mud.

More appealingly, the raised land on river left marks out Rainham Marshes, a RSPB reserve

Estuary inhabitant.

since 2000. These are part of the Inner Thames Marshes SSSI, comprising Rainham, Aveley and Wennington Marshes. This was formerly a military range. Look also for The Diver, a statue which partly covers at high tide. The river bends left opposite the town of Erith at Coldharbour Point. The tens of thousands of gulls here may be connected to the landfill site behind. Essex begins hereabouts.

On river right, the RSPB reserve at Crayford Marshes leads to Crayford Ness, marking a right bend revealing Long Reach, a five-kilo-metre straight passing beneath Queen Elizabeth II Bridge. The river right confluence of the River Darent (another tidal barrier) marks the border of Kent, and the Dartford Marshes which follow are the site of a former isolation hospital and quarantine station. This is all more attractive than it probably sounds.

📷 *Approaching Queen Elizabeth II Bridge.*

It's impossible not to feel awed and very small approaching Queen Elizabeth II Bridge, opened in 1991. It is 2,872m long and its 450m central span suspends the southbound M25 traffic 57.6m above the water; the northbound traffic is thirty metres below the riverbed in the 1963 Dartford Tunnel. Alongside is the 215m tall chimney of (decommissioned) Littlebrook Power Station, which may be demolished in the near future.

Greenhithe (river right) is an attractive eighteenth-century town. *Cutty Sark* was moored here until 1954, and Sir John Franklin left here in 1845 to search for the North-West Passage, never to return.

The UK's two tallest pylons cross 190m above St Clement's Reach, the river takes a sharp right turn around Broadness, and then the cranes of Tilbury Docks fill the sky. The docks opened in 1886, coming into their own when ships outgrew London. This is among Europe's busiest ports; keep well clear to river right.

All that remains is to follow the Gravesend waterfront past various dilapidated piers to the rowing club slipway.

The earthworks visible across the river are Tilbury Fort, described by Daniel Defoe in the 1720s as "The key to London". Henry VIII founded the fort in 1539. Tilbury was the scene of Elizabeth I's stirring "I have the heart and stomach of a king" speech, made in the face of the Spanish Armada's threat. The present fort mostly dates from the 1670s, rebuilt after the Dutch destroyed it in 1667. This was always a grim posting; in the 1870s the garrison was changed every six months due to malaria.

[📷] *Approaching Jenningtree Point.*

At the opening of *Heart of Darkness* (Joseph Conrad 1899), the narrator is moored off Tilbury at dusk. He observes that the Thames was once as wild as the Congo: "And this also ... has been one of the dark places of the earth". Experiencing the river's bleak expanses today, you can allow yourself to believe that it still is. Don't let them build an airport on it.

[📷] *Below Queen Elizabeth II Bridge.*

The Princess Alice disaster

In 1878, Tripcock Ness saw the Thames' worst shipping accident. The passenger steamer *SS Princess Alice* was making its way upriver and encountered the collier *Bywell Castle* approaching down-river. The *Alice* followed local custom by crossing to the slack water inside the bend, instead of keeping to starboard as per standard shipping protocol. This lead to the Bywell Castle ramming it amidships and severing it in two. Over 700 died; cruelly, many seem to have survived the sinking but then been poisoned by London's raw sewage, released from Crossness an hour before. Survivor Elizabeth Stride was unfortunate enough to be murdered by Jack the Ripper, a decade later.

© Gravesend.

Gravesend to Sea Reach No. 1 Buoy

38km+

△ Gravesend TQ 652 744 / DA12 2BS

○ Sea Reach No. 1 Buoy TQ 996 806 / Sheerness TQ 941 748 / ME12 2BX

Introduction

Greenwich, the Barrier (i.e. Woolwich) and Gravesend could all be regarded as appropriate places to finish an expedition down the River Thames. Some paddlers will however wish to go further and search for the river's end point. If you decide to venture this far down the estuary, sea kayaking skills and navigational expertise are needed. Summarised below is just enough information to start planning your own journey.

Launch points

Gravesend TQ 652 744 / DA12 2BS – wooden slipway on river right leading past Rowing Club to small parking area.

Sheerness TQ 941 748 / ME12 2BX – Barton's Point, Sheerness, river right side of estuary. Park atop and launch from the seawall, 2km east of Sheerness. Some mud at very low tide, but better than most of this coast!

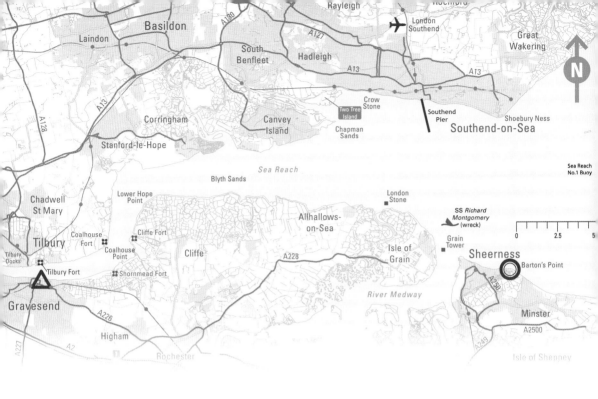

Description

Sailors judged The Nore to be the River Thames' end, a sandbank between Southend-on-Sea and the Sheerness. The 'river' is over six kilometres wide at this point!

This guidebook suggests that the precise end point is a bit further east; Sea Reach No. 1 Buoy. The 'Sea Reach' is the final stretch of the River Thames, extending seawards from Lower Hope Point to Sea Reach No. 1 Buoy. There are actually two No. 1 buoys, marking the port and starboard sides of the Yantlet Shipping Channel's entrance; this runs through the Sea Reach. The buoys are eight kilometres north-east of Barton's Point (near Sheerness in Kent) and seven kilometres south-east of Shoebury Ness (near Southend-on-Sea in Essex). They are 347 kilometres from the source, which almost agrees with Wikipedia's River Thames measurement of 346 kilometres. If anywhere is the precise end of the Thames, it has to be here!

Anyone with an ounce of sense reading this will see that the No. 1 buoys aren't a very practical place to end a Thames expedition, and are definitely not a safe one. Where would you land, having already paddled thirty-eight kilometres down-tide from Gravesend? Is it wise to be near this extremely busy shipping channel? (The simple answer is no!) Advanced sea kayaking and navigational skills and experience would be needed to safely reach this spot and even then the most obvious question remains unanswered: "Why?".

If you wish to venture this far down the Thames, your safest bet is to hug the shore and finish your Thames journey at Sheerness

📷 Near Cliffe Fort.

(south) or perhaps at Southend-on-Sea (north). Both destinations are however awkward to access due to wide expanses of mud and sand, Southend-on-Sea much more so.

The landscape below Gravesend is best described by the narrator of *Great Expectations*, Pip: "the dark flat wilderness ... was the marshes; and that the low leaden line beyond, was the river; and that the distant savage lair from which the wind was rushing, was the sea." (Charles Dickens 1861)

The beauty and monotony of this wilderness is protected by various huge nature reserves such as RSPB Shorne Marshes just after Gravesend, and Thurrock Thameside Nature Park, behind Mucking Mud Flats on the Essex shore.

The remains of various low-lying Victorian forts ('Palmerston Follies') guard the approaches to London; Shornmead Fort is followed on the south bank by Cliffe Fort, which faces Coalhouse Fort across the river, with further forts downstream around the Medway entrance.

Most noticeable is the industry; after the river bends for the last time, the Essex shore is covered for several kilometres by the sites

📷 Cliffe Fort.

of several huge refineries (oil products were not allowed upriver). The last, Coryton Refinery, closed in 2012 and the area is now a commercial port.

Continuing along the Essex shore, Canvey Island is hidden behind a sea wall, an intriguing mix of industry, static caravans and amusement arcades. The sand and mud of Hadleigh Ray separate Canvey from Southend-on-Sea; in between is uninhabited Two Tree Island, a former waste tip which has been successfully reclaimed by Essex Wildlife Trust into a nature reserve; this is linked by bridge to Leigh-on-Sea, a fishing village which retains some individual character from Southend. A couple of kilometres east of Leigh-on-Sea (TQ 857 852) the Crow Stone stands on the mud, a needle on a plinth which marked the end of the

London Corporation's jurisdiction (which lead upriver to the London Stone at Staines). The current stone dates from 1837, but there has likely been a marker here since 1285. Ahead is Southend Pier, built in 1895 and the longest in the world at 2.2km. There is a lifeboat station at the end. The mud flats around host basking grey and common seals. Shoebury Ness follows; this headland features a firing range (pointed east) and after this the mud widens much further to become Maplin Sands. Where best to land at low tide, if aiming for the Essex shore? You judge, but be sure to have a well-thought-out plan beforehand.

The Kent shore initially follows wide mud flats opposite Canvey Island. Somewhere amidst these is Yantlet Creek where the London Stone (TQ 860 786) stands. This is a twin of the Crow

 Thames Estuary.

📷 *Red Sands Fort.*

Stone (above), 6.5km north across the water. The Isle of Grain follows, before the Medway Channel opens up; take great care here as you will have to cross this shipping lane to reach Sheerness. Note the Grain Tower, a peculiar tall fort, built far out on the mud. Also note that the SS *Richard Montgomery* is hereabouts, surrounded by warning signs and buoys. This American cargo ship ran aground on The Nore sandbank in 1944, and still contains epic amounts of explosives. The suggested take-out at Barton's Point should involve only the minimum of wading through mud.

Wherever you decide to end your journey; if you reach *any* of the places mentioned in this section having paddled from the Cotswolds, then you can truly say that you have paddled the Thames.

Eight kilometres east of Sea Reach No. 1 Buoy, seven huge metal towers rear from the water. This is **Red Sands Fort**, one of the Maunsell forts built during WWII to protect London from bombers flying up the Thames. This incredible spot is described in *South East England & Channel Islands Sea Kayaking*, Derek Hairon et al., Pesda Press, 2015, ISBN 9781906095505.

Access to the Thames

"As long as the stream is navigable and no landing is attempted, the right of way cannot be disputed."

George D. Leslie, *Our River* 1888

Paddlers enjoy excellent access to all parts of the River Thames. The only restricted area on the entire river is the space in front of the Houses of Parliament, and we don't recommend entering that!

Cricklade to Teddington

There are no restrictions on paddling the Thames other than the need to register your boat with the Environment Agency; this can be done at locks or online, www.gov.uk/register-a-boat. Most paddlers join British Canoeing (formerly known as the British Canoe Union), www.britishcanoeing.org.uk. British Canoeing membership permits you to paddle a canoe on the Thames, even with other non-members on board. Simple. Lock keepers will occasionally ask you about boat registration; simply show them your membership card. The EA recommend keeping this on your person in a waterproof bag.

The Thames from Cricklade was managed by the Thames Conservancy from 1857, the National Rivers Authority from 1989 to 1996, and the Environment Agency ever since.

The Tideway

No license is required to paddle on the Thames below Teddington Lock. The tidal river has been under the jurisdiction of the Port of London Authority (www.pla.co.uk) since 1909, so you are expected (and given the challenges of this stretch, advised!) to follow their guidance (see Paddling the Tideway).

Launching at Shadwell Basin on the Tideway.

Launching on the Thames

The Thames offers numerous good spots suitable for launching canoes and kayaks. However, information about them is surprisingly hard to track down! This factor has undoubtedly discouraged many paddlers from enjoying the river in the past. The list below is by no means exhaustive, but hopefully offers a wide enough range of possibilities to give access to all sections. Marinas have not been included, being geared towards larger craft and usually involving a launch fee.

It should be noted that not all spots listed are on public land; check details in the section description.

Unfortunately, Central London completely lacks decent public access points to the river ... and that is before we mention the roads and parking! The many pontoons and piers are privately owned. However, those living in the capital's heart may wish to make use of the Thames' iconic 'steps'. These narrow passageways to the water are hidden in many useful spots. The downsides are that launching can be awkward and is tide dependent, some are in a state of decay and many are inexplicably locked. As developers encroach, these secret access points are becoming an endangered species. Thankfully, the River Thames Society www.riverthamessociety. org.uk monitors their condition and publishes a useful guide on its website: *Access to the River Thames: Steps, Stairs & Landing Places on the Tidal River.*

Waypoint	Grid reference	Post code	Possible launch point?	Distance from previous waypoint	Distance from source of Thames
Upper Thames					
Source of the Thames	ST 981 995	GL7 6NZ	N	0km	0km
Waterhay Bridge	SU 060 933	SN6 6QY	N	13.4km	13.4km
Cricklade High Bridge	SU 101 940	SN6 6DA	N	6km	19.4km
Cricklade slipway	SU 103 938	SN6 6BL	Y, RR	0.2km	19.6km
Red Lion, Castle Eaton	SU 145 958	SN6 6JZ	Y, RR	6.5km	26.1km
Hannington Bridge	SU 174 961	SN6 7RX	Y, RL	4.4km	30.5km
Lechlade Riverside Park	SU 211 990	GL7 3AL	Y, RR	6.1km	36.6km
Lechlade Riverside Inn	SU 213 994	GL7 3AQ	Y, RL	0.6km	37.2km
Trout Inn, Lechlade	SU 224 990	GL7 3HA	Y, RL	1.2km	38.4km
Cheese Wharf	SU 224 983	SN7 8DQ	Y, RR	0.8km	39.2km
Radcot Bridge	SU 285 994	OX18 2SX	Y, RL	8.1km	47.3km
Tadpole Bridge	SP 335 004	SN7 8RF	Y, RL	6.5km	53.8km
Newbridge	SP 404 014	OX29 7QD	Y, RL/RR	9.6km	63.4km
Bablock Hythe	SP 435 042	OX29 5AT	Y, RR	5.9km	69.3km
Wolvercote	SP 487 094	OX2 8PG	Y, RL	10.3km	79.6km
Osney Bridge	SP 503 062	OX2 0AU	Y, RR	5.6km	85.2km
Middle Thames					
Riverside Centre	SP 524 044	OX4 4AZ	Y, RL	3.2km	88.4km
Abingdon Bridge	SU 499 968	OX14 5EJ	Y, RL	11.7km	100.1km
Sutton Bridge	SU 508 949	OX14 3BN	Y, RL	3.5km	103.6km
Clifton Hampden	SU 547 955	OX14 3EE	Y, RL	5.1km	108.7km
Shillingford Bridge	SU 597 921	OX10 7EU	Y, RL	8.5km	117.2km
Benson	SU 614 915	OX10 6SH	Y, RL	1.8km	119km
Wallingford Bridge	SU 610 894	OX10 0BL	Y, RL	2.2km	121.2km

Waypoint	Grid reference	Post code	Possible launch point?	Distance from previous waypoint	Distance from source of Thames
Cholsey	SU 601 855	OX10 9GZ	Y, RR	4.3km	125.5km
South Stoke	SU 594 837	OX10 9JU	Y, RL	2.2km	127.7km
Goring Bridge	SU 597 808	RG8 1AU	Y, RL	3.2km	130.9km
Whitchurch Bridge	SU 636 768	RG8 7DA	Y, RR	6.7km	137.6km
Tilehurst	SU 686 746	RG30 6AY	Y, RR	6.7km	144.3km
Caversham Bridge	SU 710 746	RG1 8BD	Y, RR	2.9km	147.2km
Lower Thames					
Wokingham Waterside Centre	SU 736 740	RG6 1PQ	Y, RR	2.6km	149.8km
Wargrave	SU 786 790	RG10 8HZ	Y, RR	8.2km	158km
Marsh Lock	SU 772 818	RG9 3HY	Y, RL	3.2km	161.2km
Henley (Museum)	SU 767 821	RG9 1BF	Y, RL	0.9km	162.1km
Henley (Wharfe Lane)	SU 763 828	RG9 2LJ	Y, RL	0.7km	162.8km
Remenham	SU 770 843	RG9 3DB	Y, RR	1.7km	164.5km
Aston	SU 787 845	RG9 3DH	Y, RR	2.8km	167.3km
Medmenham	SU 806 837	SL7 2ER	Y, RL	2.5km	169.8km
Marlow	SU 852 862	SL7 1NQ	Y, RL	6km	175.8km
Bourne End	SU 884 873	SL8 5PS	Y, RL	3.7km	179.5km
Cookham Bridge	SU 898 855	SL6 9SW	Y, RR	3.4km	182.9km
Maidenhead (Boulter's Lock)	SU 902 825	SL6 8JB	Y, RR	3.2km	186.1km
Maidenhead (Riverside Gardens)	SU 902 819	SL6 8NJ	Y, RR	0.7km	186.8km
Bray	SU 903 797	SL6 2AU	Y, RR	2.4km	189.2km
Windsor Leisure Centre	SU 957 772	SL4 5HU	Y, RR	7.7km	196.9km
Runnymede NT	SU 997 731	TW19 5AE	Y, RR	8.7km	205.6km
Runnymede Pleasure Grounds	TQ 007 724	TW20 0AD	Y, RR	1.3km	206.9km
Staines (Church Island)	TQ 029 718	TW18 4XZ	Y, RL	2.6km	209.5km

Waypoint	Grid reference	Post code	Possible launch point?	Distance from previous waypoint	Distance from source of Thames
Staines (Truss's Island)	TQ 034 699	TW18 3LS	Y, RR	2.2km	211.7km
Staines (Penton Avenue)	TQ 038 698	TW18 2HG	Y, RL	0.6km	212.3km
Laleham	TQ 049 684	TW18 1UQ	Y, RL	1.9km	214.2km
Chertsey Bridge	TQ 054 666	KT16 8JA	Y, RL	2km	216.2km
Shepperton Lock (Weybridge)	TQ 074 657	KT13 8NG	Y, RR	3.1km	219.3km
Shepperton Lock (Ferry Lane)	TQ 074 659	TW17 9LQ	Y, RL	0.1km	219.4km
Walton Bridge	TQ 093 664	KT12 1BH	Y, RR	2km	221.4km
Walton (Anglers pub)	TQ 098 668	KT12 2PE	Y, RR	0.7km	222.1km
Walton (Sunbury Lane)	TQ 102 674	KT12 2JQ	Y, RR	0.7km	222.8km
Sunbury (Waterside Drive)	TQ 104 679	KT12 2JP	Y, RR	0.6km	223.4km
Sunbury (Lower Hampton Road)	TQ 115 689	TW16 5PN	Y, RL	1.5km	224.9km
West Molesey	TQ 142 693	KT8 9AZ	Y, RR	2.8km	227.7km
Thames Ditton (Swan Inn)	TQ 162 673	KT7 0QQ	Y, RR	2.8km	230.5km
Thames Ditton (Cholmley Road)	TQ 167 671	KT7 0XB	Y, RR	0.4km	230.9km
Kingston	TQ 176 678	KT6 4EU	Y, RR	1.3km	232.2km
The Tideway					
Teddington (Burnell Ave)	TQ 171 714	TW10 7YE	Y, RR	3.9km	236.1km
Teddington (Ferry Lane)	TQ 167 714	TW11 9NN	Y, RL	0.3km	236.4km
Twickenham Drawdock	TQ 164 732	TW1 3NX	Y,RL	2.2km	238.6km
Twickenham (White Swan Drawdock)	TQ 168 733	TW1 3DL	Y, RL	0.3km	238.9km
Richmond (Ham Street Car Park)	TQ 170 732	TW1 3DJ	Y, RR	0.1km	239km
Petersham (River Lane Drawdock)	TQ 178 735	TW10 7AQ	Y, RR	0.9km	239.9km

Waypoint	Grid reference	Post code	Possible launch point?	Distance from previous waypoint	Distance from source of Thames
Isleworth Drawdock	TQ 167 760	TW7 6BE	Y, RL	3km	242.9km
Kew Bridge Drawdock	TQ 190 779	W4 3NG	Y, RL	2.9km	245.8km
Grove Park Drawdock	TQ 197 774	W4 3QD	Y, RL	0.9km	246.7km
Mortlake (Ship Lane Drawdock)	TQ 204 761	SW14 7QW	Y, RR	1.3km	248km
Barnes (Small Profits Drawdock)	TQ 216 767	SW13 9QB	Y, RR	1.6km	249.6km
Chiswick Church Drawdock	TQ 216 777	W4 9BZ	Y, RL	0.9km	250.5km
Chiswick Drawdock	TQ 217 779	W4 2PW	Y, RL	0.3km	250.8km
Putney Bridge	TQ 238 758	SW15 1LB	Y, RR	3.7km	254.5km
Fulham (Broomhouse Drawdock)	TQ 253 755	SW6 3EJ	Y, RL	1.4km	255.9km
Battersea Church Drawdock	TQ 268 768	SW11 3ND	Y, RR	2.3km	258.2km
Shadwell Basin	TQ 354 805	E1W 3TF	Y, RL	11.6km	269.8km
Isle of Dogs (Millwall Slipway)	TQ 372 791	E14 3QS	Y, RL	2.7km	272.5km
Isle of Dogs (Newcastle Drawdock)	TQ 386 785	E14 3EA	Y, RL	2.5km	275km
Greenwich, Warspite Road	TQ 420 793	SE18 5NX	Y, RR	5.9km	280.9km
Woolwich (Bell Water Gate)	TQ 434 793	SE18 6DL	Y, RR	1.4km	282.3km
North Woolwich (Bargehouse Causeway)	TQ 438 799	E16 2NW	Y, RL	0km	282.3km
Erith Causeway	TQ 515 781	DA8 1SB	Y, RR	11km	293.3km
Greenhithe Causeway	TQ 588 752	DA9 9NS	Y, RL	7.9km	301.2km
Gravesend	TQ 652 744	DA12 2BS	Y, RR	8.3km	309.5km
Sheerness (Barton's Point)	TQ 941 748	ME12 2BX	Y, RR	30.5km	340km
Sea Reach No. 1 Buoy	TQ 996 806		N		347km

Radcot Bridge camping.

Camping

"We should go to bed with the swans and rise up with the larks, and cook our breakfast under the willows, and wash our dishes and ourselves in quiet, clear pools."

Joseph Pennell and Elizabeth Robins, *The Stream of Pleasure* 1891

One of the greatest pleasures of journeying on the River Thames is pulling ashore, unpacking a tent and camping for the night. This should be done at recognised campsites, as wild camping is not permitted. There are many pleasant riverside campsites along the Thames, including a number of quiet locks where it is possible to pitch a tent. Unfortunately campsites are not always evenly spaced and choices become limited (and eventually non-existent) as you close on London.

Hotel and B&B accommodation is not covered here. For ideas in this respect, the *Thames Path National Trail Companion* (National Trails Office, ISBN 9780956107442) is recommended. Below are listed campsites, hostels and 'glamping' options along or near the Thames. Most are closed over the winter months. Campsite details change more regularly than any other aspect of this guidebook's information, plus some of these sites get very busy; you are recommended to call ahead and check what is available before setting off! For further details of the Environment Agency's lock campsites, see www.gov.uk/guidance/river-thames-bridges-locks-and-facilities-for-boaters.

Name	Number on maps	Section(s)	Grid reference	Post code	Beside river? (River right, river left, lock island)	Distanc from source
Second Chance Caravan Park	1	1	SU 140 960	SN6 6SZ	Y, RL	25km
Bridge House Campsite	2	1,2	SU 213 991	GL7 3AG	N	
The Trout Inn	3	1,2	SU 223 990	SN7 8DQ	Y, RL	38.4km
The Swan Hotel	4	2	SU 286 998	OX18 2SX	Y, I	47.4km
Rushey Lock	5	2	SP 323 002	SN7 8RF	Y, RR	52.2km
The Trout Inn	6	2,3	SP 336 004	SN7 8RF	Y, RR	53.8km
Shifford Lock	7	3	SP 370 010	OX18 2EJ	Y, I	59.2km
Lincoln Farm Park	8	3	SP 396 027	OX29 7TJ	N	
Hardwick Parks	9	3	SP 390 046	OX29 7PZ	N	
Northmoor Lock Paddocks	10	3	SP 432 021	OX13 5JN	Y, RR	66.8km
The Ferryman Inn	11	3, 4	SP 434 042	OX29 5AT	Y, RL	69.3km
Pinkhill Lock	12	4	SP 440 071	OX8 1JH	Y, I	73.2km
Eynsham Lock	13	4	SP 445 087	OX8 1BY	Y, I	75.4km
Oxford YHA	14	4,5	SP 504 062	OX2 0AB	N	
Oxford Camping and Caravanning Club Site	15	4,5	SP 519 039	OX1 4XG	N	

Phone	Website/ email	Notes
01285 810675	www.secondchancetouring.co.uk	At Marston Meysey. Currently not accepting paddlers (2016), for reasons unclear.
01367 252348	www.bridgehousecampsite.co.uk	200m from river, at Lechlade.
01367 252 313	www.thetroutinn.com	At St John's Lock.
01367 810220	lm.mitchell@ntlworld.com	On ait opposite Inn, below Radcot Bridge. Limited facilities.
01367 870218	Environment Agency (see above)	No road access, limited facilities.
01367 870382	www.troutinn.co.uk	At Tadpole Bridge.
01367 870247	Environment Agency (see above)	Remotest campsite on the river! No road access, limited facilities.
01865 300239	www.lincolnfarmpark.co.uk	At Standlake, 1.6km from river.
01865 300501	www.hardwickparks.co.uk	At Standlake, 3km from river.
07961 514047	www.barefootcampsites.co.uk	Near Appleton. Glamping options available.
01865 880028		At Bablock Hythe.
01865 881452	Environment Agency (see above)	Near Farmoor. No road access, limited facilities.
01865 881324	Environment Agency (see above)	Near Swinford Bridge. No road access, limited facilities.
0870 770 5970	www.yha.org.uk	250m from river in central Oxford. 2a Botley Road. Youth hostel, no camping.
01865 244088	www.campingandcaravanningclub.co.uk	650m from the river. Beside Hinksey Stream. Camping and Caravanning Club members only.

Middle Thames

Name	Number on maps	Section(s)	Grid reference	Post code	Beside river? (River right, river left, lock island)	Distance from source
Bridge House Caravan Site	16	6	SU 548 953	OX14 3EH	Y, RR	108.7km
Day's Lock	17	6	SU 569 936	OX14 4RD	Y, I	112.9km
Bridge House	18	6	SU 596 921	OX10 7EU	Y, RL	117.2km
Benson Waterfront	19	6	SU 613 916	OX10 6SJ	Y, RL	119km
Riverside Park	20	6,7	SU 612 897	OX10 8EB	Y, RL	121.1km
Bridge Villa Caravan and Camping International	21	6,7	SU 612 895	OX10 8HB	N	
Streatley Youth Hostel	22	8	SU 591 806	RG8 9JJ	N	
Mapledurham Estate	23	8	SU 669 766	RG8 8BE	Y, I	141.2km

Lower Thames and Tideway

Name	Number on maps	Section(s)	Grid reference	Post code	Beside river? (River right, river left, lock island)	Distance from source
Swiss Farm International Camping	24	9	SU 760 836	RG9 2HY	N	
Hurley Riverside Park	25	10	SU 816 837	SL6 5NE	Y, RR	172.3km
Hurley Lock	26	10	SU 826 843	SL6 1SA	Y, I	172.4km
Longridge	27	10	SU 855 858	SL7 1RE	Y, RR	176.5km
Cookham Lock	28	10, 11	SU 905 855	SL6 9SR	Y, I	182.9km
Amerden Caravan and Camping Site	29	11	SU 913 796	SL6 0EE	Y, RL	189.8km
Laleham Camping Club	30	12, 13	TQ 052 679	TW18 1SS	Y, RL	214.8km
Chertsey Camping and Caravanning Club Site	31	12, 13	TQ 052 667	KT16 8JX??	Y, RR	215.9km
London Thameside YHA	32	15, 16	TQ 356 801	SE16 5PR	Y, RR	269.7km

CAMPING

Phone	Website/ email	Notes
1865 407725		At Clifton Hampden.
1865 407768	Environment Agency (see above)	Near Little Wittenham. No road access, limited facilities.
1865 858540	www.bridge-house.org.uk	Beside Shillingford Bridge. Camping and Caravanning Club members only.
01491 838304	www.bensonwaterfront.co.uk	At Benson.
01491 835232	www.better.org.uk	In Wallingford.
01491 836860	www.bridgevilla.co.uk	In Wallingford, 250m from the river.
870 770 6054	www.yha.org.uk	In Streatley, 350m from the river. Youth hostel, no camping.
0118 9417776	www.mapledurham.co.uk	Only by request; not always available.

Phone	Website/ email	Notes
01491 573419	www.swissfarmcamping.co.uk	Near Henley-on-Thames.
01628 823501	www.hurleyriversidepark.co.uk	Near Hurley.
01628 824334	Environment Agency (see above)	Near Hurley. No road access, limited facilities.
033 0303 0101	www.longridge.org.uk	Outdoor activity centre for youth groups, near Marlow. Bunk rooms also available.
01628 520752	Environment Agency (see above)	On Sashes Island near Cookham. No road access, limited facilities.
01628 627461	www.amerdencaravanpark.webs.com	Near Bray and Dorney.
01932 564149	www.lalehamcampingclub.co.uk	Laleham Park, Laleham.
01932 562405	www.campingandcaravanningclub.co.uk	At Chertsey Lock. Camping and Caravanning Club members only.
0845 3719756	www.yha.org.uk	In Rotherhithe. Youth hostel, no camping.

Completing the 2014 DW Race.

The Devizes to Westminster Race

"We were knackered and gutted ... but relieved that it was at an end."

Olympic rower Sir Steve Redgrave describes withdrawing from
the 2012 race, after 16.5 hours and 87 miles.

One of the more masochistic ways to experience the Thames is via the 125-mile Devizes
to Westminster International Canoe Race. While you might imagine that this extreme en-
durance event is the preserve of monomaniacal elite racers, it is actually entirely achievable
by motivated recreational paddlers. If proof were needed, this author has completed it (in
middle age, too!) and recommends it as a significant but rewarding challenge.

The Devizes to Westminster Race (the DW, pronounced 'dee-doubleyou') originated from a successful 1946 attempt — stemming from a pub bet — to row non-stop down the River Avon from Pewsey in Wiltshire to the sea. In 1948, a group of Scouts were inspired by this to take on the challenge of kayaking from Devizes to Westminster in under four days, via the Kennet and Avon Canal and River Thames. They achieved this feat in 90 hours, travelling self-sufficiently, in an era when the canal was derelict and overgrown! Numerous groups repeated the journey in 1949; the DW was born. Over subsequent decades the race evolved to encompass different boat classes, with the requirement to be self-supported being dropped in 1971, and finally, even wom-en(!) allowed to take part.

The DW starts at Devizes Wharf on the now-re-stored Kennet and Avon Canal, following this for 55 miles east over the watershed and down-hill to join the Thames at Reading. There are a mind-bending 56 portages along the canal. The second section is along 52 miles of the Thames to Teddington Lock, with a further 21 portages. The final reach is 17 miles down the Tideway to

Teddington Lock, 36 hours into the 2014 DW Race.

📷 *Author and Jen Clough crossing the finish line in 2014. Photo | Heather Rainsley.*

finish at Westminster Bridge. The logistics and organisation of the race are mind-boggling ... a small army of volunteers plan year-round to make it happen smoothly. What they achieve is remarkable; the DW is a truly unique event.

Entry

The DW of course has a huge wodge of rules and regulations, which can be pored over at www.dwrace.org.uk. To summarise the entry classes: double kayaks (K2s) or canoes (C2s) complete the 125 miles non-stop, excepting under-18s who paddle the route over four days with overnight camping stops (public school teams form the majority of entries for this class). Veteran/Junior pairings (K2/C2), single kayaks (K1s) and canoes (C1s) must also take the four-day approach. There is additionally the Endeavour class, which allows adult K2s to paddle over four days in a non-competitive challenge. Teams paddling non-stop must time their departure to catch the Tideway's ebb flow at the right time (from 108 miles away!).

Which DW event is for you? The non-stop race is the 'blue riband' event, but it has the notable disadvantage of passing the Thames in night-time darkness. The 'Endeavour' event is a great option for adults wanting the DW experience without racing pressures, and with the opportunity to soak up Thames scenery; however you still have to paddle the distance! The single events carry their own unique psychological challenge. A friend commented: "I've done it once over four days and twice non-stop. On each occasion the alternative sounded both easier and harder".

The non-stop DW record is a blistering 15 hours 34 mins, achieved in 1979. Some teams have since come close to beating this (notably a mixed pair in 2015) but in the very high water levels which aided the 1979 feat, the race is nowadays likely to be cancelled. If you're a contender for the course record, you probably already know. Mere mortals considering the DW will want to bear in mind the following key factors in a successful race.

Training

Folk have been known to complete the DW after just a few weeks of kayaking experience, but of course you will have a much greater chance of success (and much less pain) if you have trained for months ahead. A typical approach would be to paddle for an hour or so for two or three evenings a week from four to six months ahead, with a longer paddle at weekends. Over the two months prior to the DW, two series of races are held, offering a perfect opportunity to familiarise yourself with the route; the two Thameside Races are held on the Thames, and the four Waterside Races follow the canal and build up to 34 miles in length.

Support crew

These folk are 100% indispensible, an integral part of your DW effort; a team (or teams) of friends who will drive along the entire course, feeding you and keeping your spirits up. What you have to ask of them is pretty considerable

📷 *Approaching Marsh Lock.*

(and what, exactly, is in it for them?) but there is no way that you can be successful without their help. Factor their role and needs into your planning from the first instance and be very, very nice to them before, during and after the race.

What else?

You and your support crew will need to ponder numerous other factors, many of which will be unknowns and need testing out beforehand. Nutrition – what food will be palatable and keep you moving at 5 a.m.? Equipment – will you have the know-how to fix your kayak's rudder in mid-race? Clothing – assume that you'll get through at least three woolly hats each. Lighting – how will you find your way along the Thames? And so on, and so forth ...

The author's DW

When I started paddling in the '80s, you weren't a 'proper' paddler until you'd 'done' the DW. I managed to avoid it until my friend Jen dragged me along the 2014 four-day Endeavour event in her K2. I felt smug about completing this, but was in awe of those paddling the distance non-stop. I bought a cheap K2 and entered the 2015 race.

Despite not being a hugely experienced paddler, Chris was a great choice of partner; younger and fitter than me, with a calm and determined temperament. Chris's grandad had completed the DW by folding kayak in the 1950s, while in the Army's Special Forces. A seminar we attended advised us to build up to the final Waterside Race distance (34 miles) and no further. The 125 miles would just come together on the day ...

All winter, we slogged along our local river in cold, rain, wind, flood waters, tidal currents and darkness. Our biggest foe was my wobbly kayak; we were relieved when Jen loaned us her stable K2, just before the race!

The pre-race week was spent readying gear, support crew and nerves. We departed Devizes pre-dawn and over the following twelve hours, fifty miles of canal plodded past half-noticed. As the sun set, we were ejected into the (seemingly) vast Thames. Reality check – we'd paddled our furthest ever and weren't even halfway; I was unnerved! Banter and intermittent portages across lock islands' oases of light warded off the sleep monsters. Our seminar advice was spot on; we discovered that we could keep paddling ... 70 miles, 80, 90 ...

It wasn't plain sailing. A wrong turn at Cookham saw us pushed onto the chains above (lethal) Odney weir; we have no clue how we escaped. As dawn greyly emerged, our bodies began to crash. Our valiant support crew tried to force food upon us, but we'd lost our appetites and slowed badly. We kept moving by pretending that Teddington was the finish line; the tide would carry us thereafter. This was a mistake. Reaching Teddington, we found ourselves with 17 miles left and no mental reserves. We were late in the tide, meaning a demotivating muddy portage around Richmond Lock (and wobbles in the boils below).

The wheels came off. I started hallucinating* and had to step ashore. A few squares of our emergency chocolate (and Chris uttering the understated words: "We're going to finish this") worked to remarkable effect; I was able to get back in the boat and paddle. We rounded the final corner to see cheering crowds. I was shocked. My mindset was that everyone would have gone home by now. Actually our finish time of nearly 27 hours wasn't too bad, but longer than we'd assumed we'd take. We refused help lifting our boat up the steps at Westminster Bridge, and were then overwhelmed by exhaustion and culture shock; we'd paddled from rural Wiltshire to the Houses of Parliament!

This was an entirely positive experience (really!) which I'd recommend to others. We could not have started the race, let alone completed it, without help from the good

📷 *Chris Eden and Author at finish of 2015 DW Race.*
Photo | Heather Rainsley.

friends who made up our support crew. We still owe you all!

* *Subsequent to the race I was diagnosed as diabetic, among other extenuating medical circumstances.*

Windsor Castle.

Culture and Landscape: The Story of the Thames

"The Thames is no ordinary waterway, it is the golden thread of our nation's history."

Winston Churchill

More than any feature in our landscape, the River Thames tells, and is part of, England's story. There is no better way to experience this saga than from down at water level in a small boat!

Geology

The Cotswolds Hills where the Thames first emerges are composed of oolitic limestone formed through the Jurassic Period 201–145 million years ago. Oolites are small 'eggs' of calcium carbonate that precipitated as they rolled around on the margins of the shallow, tropical Tethys Ocean; a process that still occurs today in the Bahamas. This honey-coloured building stone is seen everywhere, in bridges, houses and walls.

The underlying rock remains Jurassic through the Upper and Middle Thames' course. The Upper Thames crosses younger sediments including the Oxford Clay, formed by a delta flowing into the Tethys Ocean. They are overlaid with sand and gravel, created by glacial outflow during successive ice advances over the last three million years. Gravel terraces of Cotswold limestone line the river and represent former flood plains, left high and dry as the river erodes downwards.

At Oxford, the Thames passes over a ridge of Corallian limestone, before winding across more clays towards the Chilterns. These 'younger' chalk hills were formed in the Cretaceous Period 145–66 mya, which is famed for the end of the dinosaurs and for chalk

Goring Gap.

seas which created the white cliffs of Dover. Heightened tectonic activity led to global increases in sea level and the deposition of countless millions of tiny calcium carbonate shells from coccolithophore algae; they are the 'white' of the chalk. Between Goring and Maidenhead, modern streams draining the Chilterns add dissolved calcium carbonate to the Thames; this is a hard water area!

The Lower Thames meanders across broad and extensive beds of gravel and alluvium covering the chalk. Between Maidenhead and Slough, the chalk is replaced by London Clay, a blue-brown mud formation which was created along sub-tropical shores during the early Palaeogene Period (66–23 mya). The clay is up to 200m thick and holds exceptionally important fossils of plants that were preserved after being washed into the sea; there is even evidence of crocodiles! London Clay underlies the river through to the estuary, although the North Downs which disrupt this low-lying landscape near Gravesend are Cretaceous chalk.

The course of the Thames

There has been some form of proto-Thames for about 170 million years. This flowed north-east across the Vale of St Albans, crossing modern-day Harwich to join the Rhine, discharging into the ocean somewhere to the north.

Ice sheets of the Anglian Glaciation redirected the Thames south and east through Goring Gap c.425,000 years ago. The Scheldt and Thames merged to form a vast river labelled the 'Fleuve Manche' by geologists, which scoured out the course of the English Channel. The Rhine still flowed northwards until another ice dam redirected it into the Fleuve Manche, 225,000 years ago.

Until c.5,500 BC, Britain was still connected to the continent. As the ice melted, the sea rose and the English Channel formed. Additionally, the North West of Britain has continually risen after the pressure of ice sheets was removed (the 'isostatic' effect), and the South East has slowly sunk. By 7,000 BC, the Thames' tidal limit was around Tilbury. It continued to move inland, eventually reaching Staines. Until human channelling and dredging, the Tideway was hugely more extensive than at present, braiding through vast marshlands.

History

The earliest known Thames valley inhabitants were Hominids who, 400,000 years ago, shaped the stone tools since uncovered in gravel terraces at places such as Culham. The landscape they inhabited is almost unimaginable; elephant and rhinoceros bathed in the river!

The post-Ice Age landscape of around 8000 BC saw a river much wider and more braided than at present; for example, Westminster was an island. The Mesolithic hunter-gatherers who ventured into this sub-Arctic wilderness left few traces beyond flint tools and flakes. As the climate warmed, the floodplain's forests changed from boreal

to deciduous, and from 4000 BC Neolithic farmers began clearing the plain, a process which continued to the early Bronze Age (c. 2500 BC). The number of grassland species increased, a consequence of more pronounced seasonal flooding due to these clearances; the Thames' iconic meadows originate from human activity! This farming and settlement was accompanied by an explosion of ritual monuments, in particular circular ditches known as 'causewayed enclosures'; there is an example immediately west of Rushey Weir. Archaeologists have dubbed this landscape "a ritual powerhouse".

The Bronze Age left us recognisable field systems and evidence of river trade; for example, a settlement with jetties has been excavated at Runnymede. Burial mounds such as those surviving at Port Meadow and Cock Marsh sprouted along the river terraces. Enigmatically, Bronze Age communities placed valuable items into the river. About 70% of the thousands of bronze items recovered were broken beforehand, seemingly deliberately. This was not waste disposal, but a ritual offering to the river. Large numbers of human skulls have also been retrieved, over one hundred for example at Strand-on-the-Green.

The valley was well populated by the Iron Age, with no towns but some large enclosed settlements, known as 'oppida' (Abingdon and Dyke Hills are likely candidates). Hillforts close to the river such as that at Wittenham are unusual, due to the generally low-lying surrounds.

The Romans

The Roman legacy to the Thames is very obvious; they founded London! *Londinium* was constructed c. AD 43 on a previously unsettled part of the north bank, in the vicinity of the modern-day City of London. It seems to have been completely abandoned after the Roman departure in AD 410.

The Thames was at the heart of the Roman communication network; Watling Street, Fosse Way, Ermine Street and the Icknield Way all crossed the river. However, archaeologists have only unearthed bridges at London (c. AD 47) and Staines.

The Middle Ages

During the 'Dark Ages', Saxon invaders made themselves comfortable along the river, evidenced by the many towns ending in *–ing*. Another Saxon suffix is *–ey* (Henley, Chertsey etc.), indicating an island settlement.

Oddly, Saxons ignored *Londinium*, instead after AD 500 establishing *Lundenwic* a short distance upriver. This came under repeated attack from marauding Vikings in the late ninth century. King Alfred eventually drove them back, establishing the Upper and Middle Thames as a frontier between the Danish lands to the north and Wessex to the south. *Lundenwic* was abandoned and the former Roman town revived c. AD 886, commencing 1,100 years of expansion by our capital.

After the 1066 Norman Conquest, William I rapidly established castles at crossing points, seeing the Thames as crucial to controlling his new kingdom. The first was the Tower of London, its White Tower intended to dominate, control and awe the natives. Others included Oxford, Wallingford and the most famous castle of all, Windsor.

The many religious houses located alongside the river weren't just founded to spread God's Word. Monasteries also regulated river trade and industry, building mills and weirs, charging tolls and (for example at Abingdon) engineering the river's flow and course.

In 1170 the 33-year process of building London Bridge commenced. The only crossing in London for over 500 years, it aided London's growth by controlling upriver passage. Until

Radcot Bridge, the Thames' oldest.

Hambleden Mill.

demolition in 1831, its narrow arches slowed the water, making freezing possible; the result was London's famous 'frost fairs'. Concurrently with the bridge construction, Richard I also sold the rights to the river (from Staines' London Stone to the Crow Stone at Chalkwell) to the City of London to fund his crusade; the Tideway remained under their control for 660 years until the 1857 establishing of the Thames Conservancy.

1215 saw the reluctant signing of Magna Carta by King John at Runnymede, celebrated (in hindsight) as the foundation of our modern liberties. The list of Baronial demands included: "All kydells for the future shall be removed from the Thames". This was a reference to fish weirs (a kiddell was a fish basket) interfering with navigation.

The Tudor monarchs (especially Henry VIII) established riverside Royal parks and palaces around London at Hampton Court, Kew, Richmond, Whitehall and Greenwich, utilising vast tracts of confiscated monastic land.

Other monasteries which Henry dissolved were handed out to become noble residences (e.g. Medmenham and Bisham) and Godstow was left in ruins. He waged legal war on Thames weirs during the 1530s, ostensibly as they hindered navigation, but likely because many were controlled by monasteries. Henry VIII defended the capital by building five blockhouses along the estuary, most famously at Tilbury. With the Spanish threat in mind, Elizabeth I further strengthened this vast defensive

Medmenham Abbey.

📷 *Basildon House near Goring.*

📷 *Reed cutting below Rushey Lock.*

landscape, which incidentally proved largely ineffective when the Dutch sailed up the Thames in the following century (1667).

The English Civil War (1642–9) raged fiercely around Oxford, King Charles' headquarters, with Thames bridges deliberately severed right downstream to Kingston; this damage is still visible on the Upper Thames. The Great Fire of London (1666) of course led to the building of Wren's masterpiece, St Paul's Cathedral. The following century saw the creation or rebuilding of numerous riverside mansions, surrounded by the fashion of the age, gardens tastefully landscaped to please the eye, especially by removing the sight of peasants. Nuneham Court and Culham Court are examples, as is London's celebrated Arcadian landscape.

The Industrial Age

River crafts

The Thames' watermills were its earliest mechanical industry, used for grinding flour, paper-making and beating metal.

Osier willows were harvested along the river's

length until at least the 1940s, especially from islands inaccessible to livestock. Willow harvesters lived in island huts and reached osier beds using coracles. Coppiced shoots were cut in January and fresh rods planted in February. The shoots were bundled for weaving into baskets, chair seats, eel bucks and fish traps (kiddells). The smallest rods were used to make crayfish pots.

Fishing

Industrial fishing on the Thames is not new; weirs (Old English wera – fish trap), were used since at least the Middle Ages to mass-harvest fish and eels.

"A stage is raised up like a little wooden bridge, on the downstream side of which a set of square frames like gallows is erected: up to these frames the eel-baskets are raised by small wooden windlasses."

George D Leslie, *Our River* 1888

Four hundred fishermen worked the Tideway in the 1790s, catching 50,000 fish a day. It was considered one of finest salmon rivers in the world. The poor ate salmon, along with eels (an East End delicacy!) from the market at Blackfriars Bridge. Pollution then began to destroy the Tideway fisheries; no salmon were caught after 1833, and the last shad and lamprey in 1850.

Trade and transport

From the Middle Ages, the Thames was a cargo highway extending into Gloucestershire. Timber and (until the 1980s!) coal from NE England were lugged upriver and cheese, flour, meal and malt were floated downriver. Eighteenth-century barges were typically twenty-five metres long and carried fifty to sixty tons. Propulsion came from sails and towing by horses or gangs of 'halers'.

Negotiating 'flash locks' where water was simply released in surges, was difficult and

hazardous. After 1605, the Oxford-Burcot Commission built the first 'pound' locks at Iffley, Sandford and Swift Ditch (c.1620). There were no more until the Thames Navigation Commission built Boulter's in 1772; the impetus was competition from canals. By 1809, the building of twenty-six pound locks and a towpath allowed Lechlade to London to take just five days. The Thames was also linked to the navigation network; Wey Navigation 1653, Thames Severn Canal 1789, Oxford to Birmingham Canal 1790, Kennet and Avon 1804. From 1857–66, the Thames Conservancy gained jurisdiction over the whole non-tidal river; Parliament declared: "Private interests should no longer interfere with the navigation of one of the most important highways of the kingdom". They built new cuts (e.g. Shifford) and from

 Brunel's Moulsford Railway Bridge.

1898 awarded garden prizes to lock keepers! Through the nineteenth century, the Tideway was the busiest waterway on earth, serving the largest city. This imperial trade was protected by renewal of the estuary's epic defensive landscape; 1860's French invasion scares prompted the building of expensive 'Palmerston Folly' forts including Coalhouse and Cliffe. Medieval London Bridge was replaced (1831) to allow large boats through. A bridge-building frenzy culminated in the 1894 opening of Tower Bridge; it opened 50 times a day at first! 16,000 ships moored in the Pool of London. An 1850's journalist described: "the endless vista of masts that crowded each side of the river".

From the 1840s, railways began to reduce river traffic above London (in the following century, motorways ended it completely). Tideway trade still grew, as did the ships; large docks were built on the Isle of Dogs. By the twentieth century, London had twenty-six kilometres of commercial docks. The WWII Blitz (1940–41) destroyed about a third of this. Yet trade continued to grow; 1961 was the all-time peak, with 60 million tons handled. But the vast new container ships could not navigate the Thames, and port activity shifted downriver to Tilbury and Sheerness. By the 1970s, London's Docklands were a wasteland. Rapid and dramatic cultural change followed in the 1980s; the skyscrapers of Canary Wharf were built, the warehouses were gentrified into expensive apartments and the East End's dockers virtually erased from memory.

Leisure and tourism

"I know of no other classic stream that is splashed about for the mere fun of it ... on the smallest pretext of a holiday or fine weather, the mighty population takes to boats."

Henry James, c.1900

The earliest tourists were the 'Picturesque' movement's aesthetes; William Gilpin didn't complete his guide to the Thames' beauty spots, but Samuel Ireland published *Picturesque Views on the River Thames* (1791).

The earliest rowing regattas were held on the Thames, dominated by professional watermen. The imposition of 'amateur' rules soon conveniently ensured that only the privileged could participate; the Oxford and Cambridge Boat Race originated in 1829 and Henley Regatta a decade later.

With the railways reducing river traffic from the 1840s, the river was freed up as a place of leisure. As Brunel's Great Western Railway connected small towns like Maidenhead (1838), Goring and Pangbourne (1840), Marlow (1854) and Henley (1857), they were promoted as resorts, with hotels springing up catering for middle class weekenders and day trippers from London. All hired small boats; punts, rowing boats, sailing dinghies and canoes, being united in their hatred of loud and fast steam launches. The river's beauty was celebrated by Henry Taunt's photographic guides, produced from 1871.

From c.1820, barges and steamers also carried Londoners in the *other* direction; down the Tideway to resorts such as Gravesend, to promenade along piers. In 1833 Southend's pier exceeded two kilometres in length.

The Late Victorian and Edwardian eras saw a craze for camping along the river, popularised by the 1889 publication of *Three Men in a Boat*; the number of registered boats went up 50% in 1890! Camping barges typically had two sets of oars, a sail and a cover for sleeping. Kenneth Grahame's *The Wind in the Willows* (1908) also fuelled this fad.

The leisure boaters came up against attempts by private interests and landowners to curtail access to the Thames' back channels.

"If these men had their way they would close the River Thames altogether. They actually do this along the minor tributary streams and in the backwaters. They drive posts into the bed of the stream, and draw chains across from bank to bank, and nail huge notice-boards on every tree. The sight of those notice-boards rouses every evil instinct in my nature. I feel I want to tear each one down, and hammer it over the head of the man who put it up, until I have killed him, and then I would bury him, and put the board up over the grave as a tombstone."

Jerome K. Jerome,
Three Men in a Boat 1889

Each of these attempts failed and access was won to all of the Thames' channels. The pleasure boaters and the increasingly prevalent houseboats and chalets also gradually pushed the old river industries aside. In 1885 the Thames Conservancy banned shooting between Cricklade and Teddington, as river was now "a place of public recreation and resort". Regattas were awarded precedence over river

Boulters Lock, Sunday Afternoon. Photo | Wikipedia Commons.

trade in 1894 and passenger steamers gained priority over cargo barges at Teddington and Richmond Locks in 1897; the professional watermen had been pushed aside and the non-tidal river now belonged to the leisurely classes. This heyday of Thames boating lasted until the mid-twentieth century; however the river is still predominantly used for leisure, with 22,000 registered boats in 2015.

Shiplake and Wargrave Regatta.

Canoeing and the Thames

John MacGregor popularised kayaking as a leisure activity in the mid-nineteenth century. He made adventurous tours across Europe, after testing his Rob Roy kayak on the Thames. "It was amusing to see how much interest and curiosity the canoe excited even on the Thames, where all kinds of new and old and wonderful boats may be seen." (*A Thousand Miles in the Rob Roy Canoe* 1866.)

Poet Gerard Manley Hopkins was an early convert. He relished an 1863 paddle above Oxford: "You look, contrary of course to ordinary boats, in the direction in which you are going, and move with a single paddle – a rod with a broad round blade at either end which you dip alternately on either side. The motion is Elysian."

In 1866, MacGregor founded the Royal Canoe Club at Teddington, aiming to "promote canoeing, and unite canoeists, by arranging and recording canoe voyages ... any Gentleman nominated by two members is eligible". Prince Edward was Commodore and the 'Royal' appellation was granted by Queen Victoria in 1873.

Canoeing on the Thames developed alongside the Victorian and Edwardian mania for messing about in boats. Kayaks and open canoes were both popular, often utilising sails. In 1881, US magazine *Harper's Monthly* serialised *Down the Thames in a Birch-Bark Canoe*, James S. Whitman's paddle from Oxford to London in a leaky birch-bark canoe. English paddlers often imported open canoes, although Salters of Oxford crafted many between the 1880s and the 1930s.

The inter-war period clearly saw paddlesport grow in popularity (perhaps due to new, relatively cheap, folding kayaks). The Thames was the most popular place to paddle, due to its high profile and the availability of information. Eleanor Barnes rhapsodised about religious experiences acquired in her open canoe (*As The Water Flows* 1920), Geoffrey Boumphrey more drily described a kayak expedition (*Down River* 1936), and William Bliss went further with a series of 1930's travelogues doubling as guidebooks, outlining some rather demented attempts to reach the source. 1936 saw the publication of the *British Canoe Union Guide to the Waterways of the British Isles*, giving a mile-by-mile description of the Thames. MacGregor's pastime for Royals and gentlemen was now a much more egalitarian affair and was on the brink of becoming a mass participation sport in the post-WWII years. It's not an exaggeration to say that the Thames was central to this.

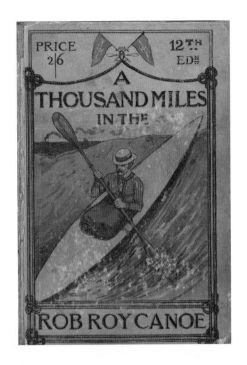

A Thousand Miles in the Rob Roy Canoe, 1866.

Heron at Shiplake.

Wildlife and Environment

"... an organic whole, in which the river and its tributaries support a vast and separate life of animals and plants ..."

C.J. Cornish, *The Naturalist on the Thames* 1902

The River Thames is immensely important as a 'wildlife superhighway' connecting much of southern England. It provides a wide variety of natural habitats, including wildflower and hay meadows, reed beds, alder and beech woodland, wet heath, chalk streams, bogland, woods and salt marshes.

Environmental issues

Despite its ecological significance, the river has historically been treated appallingly. In 1957 the Natural History Museum declared it biologically dead; through London, *nothing* lived. Its recovery in the following half-century was astonishing; it is now possibly the world's cleanest urban river, and the wildlife has largely revived accordingly.

The Upper, Middle and Lower Thames

There at least forty-six Special Protection Areas and Areas of Conservation within the basin of the non-tidal river. The Upper Thames floodplains are rated among the finest wetland areas in England and the Upper Thames Living Landscape protects 2284ha of riverside from Lechlade-on-Thames to Northmoor. Lakes formed by gravel extraction such as those in the Cotswold Water Park are now wildlife havens. Further downstream, riverside reservoirs (the Thames provides two-thirds of London's drinking water) perform a similar role. The 190+ islands are important habitats, having undeveloped banks and being inaccessible to cats and humans. The artificial Jubilee River is now a remarkably green wildlife haven; half a million trees and shrubs were planted during its creation. Undoubtedly the defining Thames environments, however, are the lush flood meadows found from Cricklade to Chertsey.

Engineering the river as a navigation has hindered nature; reinforced banks deny nesting places, while locks slow the current, reducing sediment/shingle bar habitats and limiting passage for migratory fish. Other man-made problems include urbanisation, industry, intensive farming, pollution and water abstraction; these factors are carefully monitored and regulated by the Environment Agency.

The Tideway

The entire London Thames is designated as a Site of Metropolitan Importance. It is rarely appreciated that two-thirds of London is water and green spaces, most of this being along the Thames. Over 350 species of invertebrates live on the riverbed, a sign of clean water and the basis of a healthy riverine ecosystem; fifty years ago, this was an urban sewer! The estuary below London is home to seals and other marine mammals and is surrounded by vast areas of saltings, habitat to huge populations of wading birds. This area is significantly industrialised, but this is in decline (e.g. closing refineries) and much of the land is reverting to wildness. The spectre of housing development looms, however.

Non-native species

One side effect of a cleaner Thames has been a proliferation of invasive non-native species. Japanese knotweed, giant hogweed and Himalayan balsam are all spreading along the banks. Mink have decimated voles. Signal crayfish (escaped from farms in the 1970s) are bigger and more aggressive than our native white-clawed crayfish, causing a decline in the latter; the good news is that otters find them tasty. Native mussel

populations are in sharp decline due to the impact of Asiatic species accidentally introduced from container ship ballast. Chinese mitten crabs probably arrived the same way and have been in the Tideway for around 80 years; they endanger native crabs and burrow and undermine banks.

Cleaning the Thames

The health of the River Thames is directly tied to London (and vice versa). The city's nineteenth-century growth overwhelmed the river with raw sewage, destroying fish populations. Outbreaks of cholera (a water-borne disease) killed over 40,000 Londoners from 1832 to 1866; the river was their water supply. In 1858 the 'Great Stink' led to the evacuation of parliament! Engineer Sir Joseph Bazalgette addressed these problems by building the Thames Embankments; inside these, tunnels 'captured' London's sewage and transported it downstream to Crossness and Barking. By 1865, 160km of major sewers were fed by 22,000km of smaller sewers; an epic achievement! However, the problem had just been shifted downstream, and sewage still returned on the tide. The sewers could also (and still can) be overwhelmed by heavy rain. London and the south-east's growing population put increasing pressure on the river. Descending the river by punt in 1939, Robert Gibbings described the Strand-on-the-Green foreshore: "The river is filthy ... there were children bathing, swimming in water the colour of beer, with a sediment on its surface

📷 Pangbourne Meadow.

thick enough to be the beginning of a new continent." (*Sweet Thames Run Softly* 1940) Since the London Thames was declared dead in 1957, recovery has been achieved through a range of strategies. Legislation since the 1960s has vastly reduced agricultural and industrial pollution (riverside industry is much reduced anyway). Sewage is not returned to the river; more than half is sold as agricultural fertiliser, while treatment plants clean waste water. When oxygen levels drop in the Tideway, a 'Thames Bubbler' ship pumps air into the river! Floating scoops collect litter in Central London and beach cleans by charities like Thames21 have created spaces for habitats. About 39 million tonnes of untreated sewage still overflow into the Tideway annually; Bazalgette's over-strained Victorian sewers are currently being upgraded by the Thames Tunnel Project.

Wildlife

There is so much to see and absorb, that proper justice cannot really be done here! Outlined below are some highlights of the River Thames' diverse flora and fauna.

Meadows

"*... the fields are powdered with the gold of buttercups and trefoils, the purple of clovers and vetches, the red of sorrel and the white of the ox-eye daisies ...*"

Robert Gibbings,
Sweet Thames Run Softly 1940

The wide flood meadows of the River Thames are an ancient but nonetheless man-made habitat, created by prehistoric clearance of deciduous woodlands. They are among the UK's most biodiverse grasslands, offering a haven for wild flowers, insects and mammals. They also regulate the river's flow and hold back flood waters. They have been farmed for centuries, providing both hay and livestock pasture. The most pristine meadows are above Oxford, where they are often low-lying and viewable from water level. Downstream, much has been lost to modern farming methods and urban expansion, but meadows survive as far as Chertsey.

The meadows flood in winter months, offering a habitat to redshank, curlew and snipe. From April, wild flowers and grasses proliferate. Here are just a few examples; burnt orchid, buttercup, dandelion, early marsh orchid, flag iris, great burnet, green winged orchid, marsh marigold, meadowsweet, purple loosestrife, quaking grass, ragged robin and willowherb! Most famous is the now-rare snake's head fritillary which flowers in April, distinctive due to its hanging pink and white chequered flowers. In summer, the grass is harvested for hay and cattle are grazed.

River plants

The marshy reed and sedge beds found along the Thames' fringes are rare habitats in the UK, many having been lost due to draining of land for agriculture. These beds are the haunt of water voles, warblers, kingfishers, dragonflies and damselflies. They also filter impurities from the water. The Lodden lily is found here; known as the 'summer snowflake', it is about 60cm high, its white drooping flowers appearing in April and May.

Ninety-seven percent of London's reed and sedge beds have been lost, but the decline has been reversed by replanting. Further

Snake's Head Fritillary. Photo | Wikimedia Commons.

down in the estuary, the expanses of saltings (land regularly covered by the tide) support sea meadow grass and marsh samphire, with sea lavender occupying higher parts.

Trees

"Willows, alders and poplars skirt the banks, and send their contorted roots into the stream; while their reflected forms and colours mingle with the hue imparted to the water by the tints of the sky."

James Thorne,
Rambles by Rivers 1849

The predominant riverside trees are ash, alder and willow, all of which thrive in wet ground. They stabilise the riverbank from erosion, many having been deliberately planted for this purpose.

The Chilterns and Berkshire Downs between Goring and Maidenhead give rise to chalk woodlands, composed of beech trees. The beech's overlapping leaves deprive the woodland floor of light, but fungi thrive on the leaf litter and the pallid-looking bird's nest orchid feeds parasitically off beech roots.

Willows

The willow, found atop riverbanks from the Cotswolds to London, is the Thames' defining tree. Boating on the river inspired William Morris' iconic 'Willow Boughs' wallpaper design. However, it should be noted that there are many species of willow; the main native species are the crack, goat, osier, pussy (aka sallow) and white willow. The most recognisable species, the 'weeping' willow, is a foreign introduction, the first reputedly planted in the early eighteenth century by Alexander Pope at his Richmond villa.

Fish

There are now at least 150 different fish species in the Thames; an amazing recovery. The main species found in the non-tidal Thames are bream, brown trout, bullhead, chub, dace, perch, pike and roach. The last Thames salmon was caught in 1833; these migratory fish are so sensitive to water quality that when one was again caught in 1974, it was dismissed as a practical joke. However, they really have returned and research suggests that they are freely shifting to the Thames from other catchments, and that a large reintroduction effort has actually had little effect.

Eels

The Thames is famous for its eels; jellied eel is a traditional East End dish still eaten today, presumably by those with iron stomachs. The eels arrive as larvae ('elvers') from the mid-Atlantic Sargasso Sea. They move upriver in May and June. They stay for twenty years, growing to about a metre in length, before returning downriver in October and November and swimming 6,500km back across the Atlantic to their spawning grounds.

This incredible fish is unfortunately registered as 'critically endangered'; Thames populations have crashed by 98% since the 1980s. The reasons are unclear but may relate to habitat loss and barriers to migration in the river; efforts are underway to mitigate these factors.

Mammals

Mammals living along the riverbanks include otters, water voles and water shrews. From dusk, they are joined by bats hunting for insects; seven species including Daubenton's, noctule and pipistrelle are found along the river.

Otters

"Winding in and out like an Indian in his canoe, perhaps traces of an otter might be found."

Richard Jefferies,
The Modern Thames 1884

Otters are returning! The use of organochlorine pesticides annihilated them in southern

Otter. Photo | Wikimedia Commons.

England by the end of the 1970s, but these wonderful sleek predators are now fully re-established in the Upper Thames, with regular sightings along the entire non-tidal river. In 2006, an otter came ashore at Shadwell Basin (it was sadly run over), the first seen in Central London for a century! While paddling, scan the banks for signs of their holts; these are underground resting places hidden beneath tree roots and foliage. Otters are territorial and return to these holts from a home range spanning up to 40km of river. Otters are most active nocturnally, with the best chance of seeing them being at dusk or dawn. This author has spotted one in daylight, swimming among reeds above Lechlade.

Water voles

'Ratty' of *The Wind in the Willows* can be recognised by his blunt, rounded nose, short hairy tail and small, covered ears. He is found throughout the Thames, including London; look for multiple holes tucked into riverbanks. Unfortunately he is the UK's most endangered mammal. The population dropped by 90%

during the 1990s, mainly due to mink attacks. Water voles were awarded full protected status in 2008 and a reintroduction on the Upper Thames since 2004 (along with a mink trapping program) has seen some success. The recovery of otters is also good news, as they frighten the mink away.

Marine mammals

Seals are a commonplace sight on the Tideway below London, hauled out basking on the mud flats, and occasionally entering the water to fish. They are also regularly seen as far upstream as Waterloo Bridge. At time of writing, a grey seal 'George' is a regular at the dock beside Billingsgate Fish Market, for obvious reasons.

A 2015 survey of the estuary estimated that 660 common seals and 500 grey seals lived in the greater Thames estuary. Sixty to seventy common seals were believed to breed in the Tideway above Sheerness. Identifying which type is which can be difficult (especially when you factor in age and gender), but generally common seals are smaller and have puppy-like

Water Vole. Photo | Wikimedia Commons.

Common seal near Dartford.

WILDLIFE AND ENVIRONMENT

facial features, and grey seals are larger (and fatter!) and have straight noses leading from the top of their heads to their nostrils.

Through summer and autumn, dolphins and porpoises are commonly seen in the estuary, and they have been reported as far upstream as Kew Bridge! In 2006, a Northern bottlenose whale made the headlines when it swam into Central London. It did not survive, but it gained more publicity than the much larger humpback whale which washed ashore at Dartford a few years later.

Birds

Several books could be (and have been) written about the huge and diverse birdlife along the Thames; outlined below are just a few of the author's favourites. The most visible birds are the waders, wildfowl and other wetland birds which nest, breed and swim along the river and its surrounding gravel lakes. There are numerous species but the most common include coot, cormorant, curlew, great crested grebe, mallard, moorhen, mute white

Coots.

swan, redshank, reed warbler, sedge warbler and snipe. Many nest on the Thames' islands, be careful approaching these in spring. There are many more species of waders along the Tideway, twelve appearing in 'internationally important' numbers.

Owls hunt the shores by night. Sand martins nest in burrows along the banks; in London, the lack of this habitat has been addressed by building artificial martin nests on islands.

Common terns

These are a common sight, recognisable by their forked tails and orange-red bills, and especially by their screeching, hovering and diving. Before nineteenth-century engineering of the river, they nested on gravel banks in the river and were known as 'salmon birds' as their annual return from Africa foretold the salmon run. They now nest on islands, gravel lakes and even Tideway piers.

Coots and moorhens

These rotund chaps can regularly be spotted splashing around reeds and lily pads where they nest and lay eggs. Moorhens are the ones with red beaks, coots have white beaks. The chicks of both are scrawny fur balls, moorhen chicks having bright red heads. The chicks become independent after two months, at which point their parents lay a second clutch of eggs.

📷 *Greylag geese.*

📷 *Kingfisher. Photo | Wikimedia Commons.*

Geese

Brent, Canada, greylag and the more ex-otic-appearing Egyptian geese all feature, roosting in huge numbers on the Middle and Lower Thames; encountering hundreds at once is normal. They have few predators and can produce four or five young annually; their populations have increased to the point where some regard them as a pest. Paddlers will become very familiar with their ubiquitous turds.

Grey heron

It is easy to pass Thames herons unnoticed, despite their ninety-centimetre height. They stand motionless over eddy-lines and weir pools looking for fish, their white underside and blue-grey back seeming to blend into any background. Often you hear their call, *"frank"* before they reveal themselves by taking off with their distinctive slow flapping. Heronries (breeding grounds) are found in treetops and reed beds; Thames islands are particularly favoured spots. Herons understandably disappeared from London when the fish died. Now they are back in force, as anyone who has paddled around islands like Brentford Ait can attest.

Kingfishers

Improvement of riverside habitats has lead to increased numbers of kingfishers, now an everyday sight. Canoeist Eleanor Barnes wrote "… flashing straight down mid stream at lightning speed, a thought from God, gleaming to brown eternity, or facing up stream, shows brave orange breast, beak scarlet lined, the little body full of dash and life, cloaked with unspeakable blue, sparkling with colour as with jewels not to be described." (*As The Water Flows* 1920)

Mute swans

"I don't like swans. I think they are self-opinionated and cantankerous …"

Robert Gibbings,
Sweet Thames Run Softly 1940

Thames swans, historically a delicacy, belong to the Monarch ('Seigneur of the Swans'). For 700 years, the Swan Upping ceremony has taken place in July, a census of the population between Sunbury and Abingdon. 'Upping' is removing them from the river. The scarlet-uniformed Queen's Swan Warden and Royal Swan Uppers (I don't make this stuff up) row up-

Red kites

Reintroduced red kites are a commonplace of the Middle Thames landscape. They wheel above the riverbank, emitting high-pitched calls while scanning for carrion and prey. With their 170cm wingspan, forked tails and red-brown colouring, they are impossible to mistake.

stream in skiffs for five days, while measuring, weighing and tagging each swan encountered. There were 1,200 swans in the 1950s, but by the late 1980s only seven broods survived between Henley and London. Swans delve for grit to grind down weeds in their gizzard, and were swallowing fishermen's discarded poisonous lead weights. Their deaths were distressing; muscle wastage meant that they eventually couldn't raise their necks to feed themselves. In 1987, lead weights were banned and numbers have since recovered; 2,014 swans in 2014! Discarded line and hooks remain a major problem however.

Peregrine falcons

Although the Thames hosts only a handful of pairs of this 250kph raptor, their presence is something special! In recent years they have established nests on high points above the river in Central London, favouring the Tate Modern's chimney, the Houses of Parliament and the O2 Arena's supporting towers! Lucky paddlers will spy them hunting against the capital's skyline.

Rose ringed parakeet

These exotic bright green birds can be enjoyed along the Thames through London, with hundreds congregating together at dusk. Spoiler alert – they're not native! It's rumoured that they were originally released in the 1960s by Jimi Hendrix. Another story is that they escaped in 1951 during Shepperton Studios' filming of *The African Queen* at Brentford Ait.

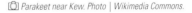
Parakeet near Kew. Photo | Wikimedia Commons.

Further Reading

"There are almost as many books about the Thames as there are about love. There will always be more; for the river is always changing its clothes."

Alan Patrick Herbert, *The Thames* 1966

Useful books

Arcadian Thames: the river landscape from Hampton to Kew, Mavis Batey et al., Barn Elms, 2000, ISBN 1899531076

Exploring the Thames Wilderness: A guide to the natural Thames, Richard T. Mayon-White and Wendy Yorke, Adlard Coles Nautical, 2013, ISBN 9781408181126

Eyots and Aits: Islands of the River Thames, Miranda Vickers, The History Press, 2012, ISBN 9780752462134

Front-Line Thames, Michael Foley, History Press, 2013, ISBN 9780750950503

I Never Knew That about the River Thames, Christopher Winn, Ebury, 2010, ISBN 9780091933579

London River, Gavin Weightman, Collins and Brown, 1990, ISBN 9781855850750

London's Thames, Gavin Weightman, John Murray, 2004, ISBN 0719564115

Rivers, Nigel Holmes and Paul Raven, British Wildlife Publishing, 2014, ISBN 9780956490254

River Thames: In the Footsteps of the Famous, Paul Goldsack, Bradt, 2003, ISBN 1841620440

Searching the Thames, Priscilla Waugh, Aurum Press, 1999, ISBN 1854106201

Southern England, Peter Friend, Collins New Naturalist, 2008, ISBN 9780007247431

Thames: Sacred River, Peter Ackroyd, Vintage, 2008, ISBN 9780099422556

The Middle and Lower Thames – A Pictorial History, Josephine Jeremiah, Phillimore & Co. Ltd, 2009, ISBN 9781860775833

The River – The Thames in our Time, Patrick Wright, BBC Worldwide, 1999, ISBN 0563384786

The Story of the Thames, Andrew Sargent, Amberley, 2013, ISBN 9781445611945

The Thames, Derek Pratt, Adlard Coles, 2008, ISBN 9780713688320

The Thames: A Cultural History, Mick Sinclair, Oxford University, 2007, ISBN 9780195314922

The Thames: England's River, Jonathan Schneer, Little and Brown, 2005, ISBN 9780316861397

The Thames from the Source to the Sea, Paul Atterbury and Anthony Haines, Weidenfeld and Nicolson, 2002, ISBN 9781841881751

The Upper and Middle Thames – A Pictorial History, Josephine Jeremiah, Phillimore & Co. Ltd, 2007, ISBN 9781860774607

Watching Wildlife in London, Marianne Taylor, New Holland, 2010, ISBN 9781847735201

Wild about the Thames, Andrew Wilson, Unity, 2010, ISBN 9780954904999

Wild London, Iain Green, Tiger Books, 2005, ISBN 0954311515

Writing the Thames, Christina Hardyment, Bodleian Library, 2016, ISBN 9781851244508

A journey down the Thames is arguably enhanced by knowing what earlier folk experienced, and how they viewed the river. The following accounts are among those cited in this guidebook:

A New Map of the River Thames, Henry Taunt, 1871

As The Water Flows, Eleanor Barnes, 1920

A Thousand Miles in the Rob Roy Canoe, John MacGregor, 1866

Canoeing, William Bliss, 1934

Dickens Dictionary of the Thames, Charles Dickens, 1887

Down River, Geoffrey Boumphrey, 1936

Down the Thames in a Birch-Bark Canoe, James S. Whitman, 1881

Our River, George D Leslie, 1888

Picturesque Views on the River Thames, Samuel Ireland, 1791

Rambles by Rivers, James Thorne, 1849

Sweet Thames Run Softly, Robert Gibbings, 1940

The Book of the River Thames, Mr and Mrs S.C. Hall, 1859

The Heart of England by Waterway, William Bliss, 1933

The Historic Thames, Hilaire Belloc, 1907

The Modern Thames, Richard Jefferies, 1884

The Naturalist on the Thames, Charles John Cornish, 1902

The Royal River – The Thames from Source to Sea, Various authors, 1885

The Stream of Pleasure, Joseph Pennell and Elizabeth Robins, 1891

The Thames: Oxford to its Source, Paul Blake, 1888

Three Men in a Boat, Jerome K. Jerome, 1889

The Wind in the Willows, Kenneth Grahame, 1908

Index